THE NEW
PRESSURE
COOKER
COOKBOOK

THE NEW
PRESSURE
COOKER
COOKBOOK

A Tantalizing Collection of Over 175 Delicious Recipes for Quick, Easy & Healthy Meals

Jake Grogan

CIDER MILL PRESS

BOOK PUBLISHERS
KENNEBUNKPORT, MAINE

13-Digit ISBN: 9781604337150
10-Digit ISBN: 160433715X

This book may be ordered by mail from the publisher. Please include $5.99 for postage and handling.
Please support your local bookseller first!

Books published by Cider Mill Press Book Publishers are available at special discounts for bulk purchases in the
United States by corporations, institutions, and other organizations. For more information, please contact the publisher.

Cider Mill Press Book Publishers
"Where good books are ready for press"
PO Box 454
12 Spring Street
Kennebunkport, Maine 04046

Visit us on the Web!
www.cidermillpress.com

Special thanks to Whalen Book Works.
www.whalenbookworks.com

WHALEN
BOOK·WORKS

NEW YORK CITY, NEW YORK

Cover and interior design by Alicia Freile, Tango Media
Page layout by Corinda Cook, Tango Media
Typography: Avenir, Fairfield, Fenway Park, Gotham, Journal, Linotype Centennial,
Minion, Neo Retro Draw, and Influence Medium

All images used under official license from Shutterstock.com.

Printed in China

1 2 3 4 5 6 7 8 9 0
First Edition

Cover Image: See page 154 for Sweet Barbecue Pork recipe.

For Danny

CONTENTS

INTRODUCTION

CAN QUALITY COOKING REALLY BE THIS EASY?

Hopefully that's the prevailing question that you come away with after enjoying some of the recipes this book has to offer; it's certainly what I came away asking myself after writing it! Here we have a wide variety of options, from stock to salmon, that take less than 30 minutes to make and yield a beautiful and delicious final product. I hope to provide busy people with easy ways to enjoy a quality meal without breaking the bank. Allocation of time is a challenge. From professional responsibilities to maintaining a social life to enjoying a little bit of downtime for yourself, activities like cooking often fall by the wayside pretty quickly. Why not spend a few extra dollars on a pressure cooker to avoid the hassle of working in a kitchen for hours to prepare a great meal?

The pressure cooker makes cooking more accessible, as it allows us to get the kind of meal we're looking for without sinking too much of our precious time into making it. These recipes were created with that function in mind. From soups and starters to larger meals that are rich in flavor and easy on the wallet, there is no audience that this book isn't appropriate for…

… Which brings me to all of my friends with dietary restrictions. Fear not! This book features plenty of vegetarian options and vegan alternatives that are just as delicious and easy to make. Gluten-free and Paleo alternatives are offered throughout as well! Nobody should feel excluded because of their dietary restrictions or choices. Ingredients can be swapped out easily enough. There's always a similar alternative, and I've done my best to note those alternatives wherever possible.

Here is the perfect mix of diet-friendly, varied, and easy-to-make recipes and flavors that all make cooking a rewarding option for everybody! Not only will these recipes produce delicious meals for the whole family, but they will also inspire creativity that will encourage you to create recipes of your own. After all, there are endless combinations out there still waiting to be discovered!

ICONS GUIDE

GO VEGETARIAN!

GO VEGAN!

GO GLUTEN-FREE!

GO PALEO!

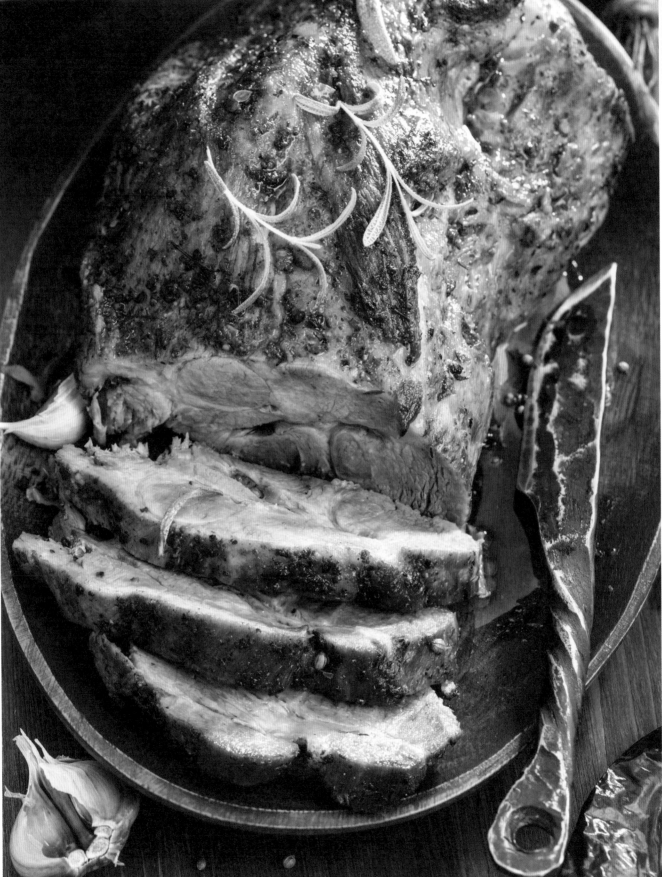

SAFETY

Ok, here we go. The one part of the book that you CANNOT skip. This is where we talk about how to use your pressure cooker! We'll break it down in list form, starting with:

1. READ THE MANUAL. If you lost it, look up the manual for your model online. All pressure cookers are a little bit different, making it impossible for me to give 100% of my instructions to fit each and every pressure cooker. You need to know how big your cooker is, how long it takes to release pressure, and the minimum amount of liquid you need for the whole thing to work. Speaking of which…

2. NEVER COOK WITHOUT LIQUID. It doesn't have to be plain old water. If you're cooking with broth or stock and the amount called for in the recipe meets or exceeds the minimum your pressure cooker needs to work, perfect. If the recipe calls for less liquid than necessary, you have to add water to it until it meets your pressure cooker's requirements. I can't stress this enough, NEVER cook in a sealed pressure cooker without having the minimum amount of liquid in there with everything else.

3. ONLY SEAL THE COOKER WHEN THE RECIPE CALLS FOR IT. A lot of recipes in here will have you browning meat or cooking onions before you actually use the pressure function of the cooker. DO NOT close the lid in these circumstances. There is no need to and it could actually damage your cooker.

4. KNOW THE MAX FILL LINE. Different sized cookers obviously have different max fill lines, so it is important that you know where it is so that you can keep it in mind when preparing a recipe. Some of the smaller cookers may need to reduce the serving size in some of these recipes in order to fit everything in one go. Generally speaking, you should not fill most cookers more than ⅔ full with liquid because there needs to be room left for the steam to build.

That said, you should have specific knowledge regarding how much liquid and food your pressure cooker can hold at any one given time.

5. Most recipes in this book will include a sentence somewhere that reads "select the High Pressure function and let cook for X number of minutes." Keep in mind that the cooking time begins once whatever pressure was selected has been achieved. So, you're not cooking for 3 minutes after selecting High Pressure, you're cooking for 3 minutes once that High Pressure has been achieved. Every electronic pressure cooker that I've dealt with didn't actually start the timer until that was the case, though you should still check to make sure yours does the same!

6. Know how to perform a quick and natural release and how to detect whether the pressure has been fully removed from your cooker. This is another area of differentiation between pressure cookers, making it extremely important that you know how to work your own.

7. CHECK TO MAKE SURE STEAM IS REMOVED BEFORE OPENING. Electrical pressure cookers handle this job on their own. However, you will have to check manually on the stovetop models. Depending on the model that you have, you're either going to jiggle the pressure regulator or the valve stem. No sound of escaping steam means that there is no more pressure in the cooker.

STOCKS & SAUCES

Here is where we will begin the not-so-daunting process of creating our very own recipe essentials! This book includes quite a few recipes that are dependent on some of what we will be making in this section. Quick, easy and budget-friendly, this section epitomizes what makes the pressure cooker such an amazing tool. Everything we make here can be made in large quantities and stored for future use, so frequent pressure cooker users would do well to familiarize themselves with the stocks and sauces detailed here. Of course, following all of these recipes yields a final product that can be easily purchased in most any grocery store. So, if you would like to skip this section to get to the starters (entrees? desserts!?) you won't be disappointed. Let's not forget the sauces! The latter half of this section features some sauce recipes that, like the stocks, can be used later on in the book. Even sauces like the Herbed Italian Sauce, despite there being few pasta dishes in this book, can find a home on the mini turkey meatballs.

BEEF STOCK

MAKES 4 QUARTS ✦ PREP TIME: 15 MINUTES ✦ COOKING TIME: 1 HOUR 10 MINUTES

Perfect for any recipe including meat, this stock is full of flavor and well worth making for future use!

1 tablespoon vegetable oil

4 quarts water

4 pounds beef shanks

2 celery ribs, sliced

2 onions, sliced

2 large carrots, peeled and thinly sliced

2 teaspoons whole black peppercorns

6 cilantro sprigs

5 teaspoons dried basil

1 bay leaf

1. Stovetop pressure cooker: Place over medium heat. Add oil. Electrical pressure cooker: Select the Sauté function. Add oil.

2. Once hot, add half of the beef to the cooker. Cook for about 4 minutes per side, or until browned, remove and set aside, and repeat with the other half of the beef.

3. Place the celery, onions, and carrots in the pot and cook for 5 minutes. Return the beef to the cooker and add water. Seal the cover, select the High Pressure function and, if using a stovetop cooker, lower the heat as much as possible while maintaining the high pressure. Allow to cook for 55 minutes.

4. Use the natural release method and slowly remove the lid once the pressure has left the cooker. Remove the beef and set aside. Pour the remaining contents through a strainer into a container, separating the stock from everything else.

Tip! – If you want to remove the fat from your broth, simply refrigerate for 48 hours. The fat will float to the top, making its removal simple and quick.

GO PALEO! Replace the vegetable oil with avocado, olive, or coconut oil.

CHICKEN BONE BROTH

MAKES 4 QUARTS ✦ PREP TIME: 5 MINUTES ✦ COOKING TIME: 30 MINUTES

Like the beef stock, a chicken broth is an essential foundation that will enhance the flavor of any dish!

1 tablespoon apple cider vinegar

½ chicken, thawed

2 ribs celery, chopped

2 cloves garlic, minced

1½ tablespoons sea salt

1 carrot, chopped

1 tablespoon chopped parsley

1 tablespoon chopped parsley

4 quarts water

1. Place all of the ingredients into the pressure cooker, filling it with water up to the max fill line. Seal the cover, select the High Pressure function, and let cook for 30 minutes.

2. Use the natural release method, slowly removing the lid once the valve has dropped. Remove the chicken from the broth and set aside.

3. Strain the liquid in the pressure cooker into a container in order to separate the bone broth from the vegetables. Use for soup immediately or store for later use.

FISH STOCK

MAKES 4 QUARTS ✦ PREP TIME: 10 MINUTES ✦ COOKING TIME: 1 HOUR 10 MINUTES

Not to state the obvious, but this stock is perfect for any seafood dish! I prefer the fish stock, but the seafood stock (see the Go Paleo option below) is just as flavorful and is preferred by many.

1 tablespoon vegetable oil

4 large salmon heads, quartered

4 quarts water

1 cup white wine

4 lemongrass stalks, chopped

2 carrots, sliced

2 celery ribs, chopped

4 cloves garlic, peeled

2 tablespoons black peppercorns

2 teaspoons dried thyme

6 parsley sprigs

1 bay leaf

1. Wash the fish heads with water, removing any visible blood!

2. Stovetop Pressure Cooker: Place over medium heat. Add oil. Electric Pressure Cooker: Select the Sauté function. Add oil.

3. Once hot, place two of the salmon heads into the pressure cooker and sear on each side for 2 minutes. Repeat this process with the remaining salmon heads.

4. Add the remaining ingredients to the cooker, seal it, select the Soup function and let cook for 45 minutes on high pressure. Cook for 45 minutes over medium heat if using a stovetop cooker.

5. Use the natural release method and slowly remove the lid once the pressure has left the cooker. Remove the fish heads and set aside. Pour the remaining contents of the cooker through a strainer to separate the stock. Use immediately or store in freezer for later use.

Replacement! – *If you're more of a shellfish person, fear not! The salmon heads can be replaced with full body lobster shells sans tail and claw meat.*

GO PALEO! Replace the vegetable oil with avocado, olive, or coconut oil.

VEGETABLE STOCK

MAKES 4 QUARTS ✦ PREP TIME: 10 MINUTES ✦ COOKING TIME: 15 MINUTES

You'll find this stock mentioned a lot throughout the book, as it is a necessary substitute in making recipes vegetarian or vegan. If you fall under one of those two categories, I would strongly recommend familiarizing yourself with this recipe.

4 quarts water

2 onions, thinly sliced

4 celery ribs, chopped

4 cloves garlic, peeled

4 carrots, sliced

2 tablespoons peppercorn

2 teaspoons dried basil

3 sprigs parsley

1 bay leaf

1. Place all of the ingredients into the pressure cooker, seal shut, select the High Pressure function. Cook for 15 minutes.

2. Use the natural release method and slowly remove the lid once the pressure has left the cooker. Pour the contents through a strainer to separate the stock from the vegetables.

Tip! – The stock can be stored in a refrigerator for up to 4 days or a freezer for up to 6 months.

BROCCOLI PESTO

MAKES 2 CUPS ✦ PREP TIME: 10 MINUTES ✦ COOKING TIME: 3 MINUTES

I'm a big fan of broccoli pesto, but this recipe can be made just as easily with a different vegetable or herb, like cauliflower or basil!

¾ pound broccoli, stemmed

2 cups water

2 cloves garlic, minced

2 tablespoons olive oil

1 cup basil leaves

½ lemon, juiced

¼ cup Parmesan cheese, grated

Salt and pepper to taste

1. Place the broccoli and water into the pressure cooker, seal, and select the High Pressure function. Cook for 3 minutes.

2. Use the quick-release method and slowly remove the lid once the pressure has left the cooker. Strain the contents of the cooker into a separate container and rinse the broccoli.

3. Place the broccoli into a food processor, along with the garlic, olive oil, basil leaves, and lemon juice. Blend until well mixed. Add cooking liquid until desired consistency is achieved, and then season with Parmesan cheese, salt, and pepper to taste.

GO VEGAN AND PALEO!   Swap the Parmesan cheese in this recipe with a non-dairy substitute for Parmesan cheese.

HOMEMADE KETCHUP

MAKES 5 CUPS | **PREP TIME: 10 MINUTES** | **COOKING TIME: 30 MINUTES**

A kitchen essential, this ketchup is practical and easy to make. It also makes for easy storage, so consider future use when deciding whether or not to make it!

4 tablespoons olive oil

1 large onion, chopped

7 garlic cloves, minced

3 pounds plum tomatoes, quartered and crushed

1½ tablespoon paprika

1 cup red wine vinegar

⅔ cup brown sugar

½ teaspoon pepper

1 teaspoon salt

½ teaspoon celery seeds

1. Stovetop Pressure Cooker: Place over medium heat. Add oil
Electrical Pressure Cooker: Select the Sauté function. Add oil.

2. Once hot, place the chopped onion into the pressure cooker and cook for 3 minutes.

3. Add the garlic, tomatoes, paprika, vinegar, sugar, pepper, salt and celery seeds to the cooker, seal the lid, select the High Pressure function and let cook for 17 minutes.

4. Use the natural release method and slowly remove the lid once the pressure has left the cooker. Stir the contents of the cooker, add salt and pepper to taste, and let simmer uncovered for 10 minutes.

5. Empty the ketchup into a food processor and blend until smooth. Serve at room temperature or store in the refrigerator for later use.

Tip! – Stores in a refrigerator for up to a month or a freezer for up to 3 months.

GO PALEO! Replace the ⅔ cup brown sugar with ⅓ cup natural maple syrup.

MARINARA SAUCE

MAKES 4 CUPS ✦ PREP TIME: 10 MINUTES ✦ COOKING TIME: 32 MINUTES

A worthy sauce in any kitchen, this marinara sauce features just the right amount of garlic which, in turn, does well to complement the tomatoes and onions!

2 tablespoons olive oil

1 medium onion, finely chopped

¼ cup red lentils

4 garlic cloves, minced

2 tomatoes, quartered and crushed

1 cup water

½ teaspoon dried oregano

Salt and pepper to taste

1. Stovetop Pressure Cooker: Place over medium heat. Add oil
   Electrical Pressure Cooker: Select the Sauté function. Add oil.

2. Once hot, place the chopped onion into the pressure cooker and cook for 3 minutes. Add the lentils and garlic and cook for another minute.

3. Add the tomatoes, water, and oregano to the cooker, seal shut, select the High Pressure function, and let cook for 25 to 30 minutes.

4. Use the natural release method and slowly remove the lid once the pressure has left the cooker. Stir well and add salt and pepper to taste.

5. Place contents of the cooker into a food processor and blend until smooth.

Tip! – Keeps up to 1 week in the refrigerator or 3 months in the freezer.

CRANBERRY SAUCE

MAKES 2 SERVINGS ✦ PREP TIME: 5 MINUTES ✦ COOKING TIME: 15 MINUTES

Who says that cranberry sauce can only be served on Thanksgiving?

24 ounces cranberries (about 2 cups), rinsed

1 piece ginger, sliced

2 cups fresh orange juice

1 cup sugar

1. Add all of the ingredients to the pressure cooker, seal shut, select the High Pressure function, and let cook for 15 minutes.

2. Use the natural release method and slowly remove the lid once the pressure has left the cooker.

3. Let cool for several minutes before serving.

Tip! – This dish can be stored in the refrigerator for up to 3 weeks.

APPLESAUCE

MAKES 6 SERVINGS ✦ PREP TIME: 2 MINUTES ✦ COOKING TIME: 4 MINUTES

Let's be honest, applesauce is one of the greatest sauces of all time! Be sure to serve it alongside any dish that calls for pork, since pork and applesauce are a match made in heaven.

12 large red apples, peeled, cored, sliced and quartered

½ cup all natural apple juice

¼ cup sugar

2 drops cinnamon essential oil

1½ teaspoon cinnamon, ground

1. Place all ingredients in the pressure cooker and mix together. Select the High Pressure function and let cook for 4 minutes. Use the natural release method and slowly remove the lid once the pressure has left the cooker.

2. Stir the applesauce well before removing from the cooker. Once your desired consistency is achieved, the applesauce will be ready to serve.

Tip! – If you subscribe to the gluten-free diet, make sure the cinnamon oil and ground cinnamon are gluten-free before purchasing.

GO PALEO! Replace the sugar with half the quantity of honey.

ONION GRAVY

MAKES 2 CUPS ✦ PREP TIME: 15 MINUTES ✦ COOKING TIME: 18 MINUTES

You really can't go wrong serving this over a meat dish when you need a boost of flavor!

1 tablespoon olive oil

1 yellow onion, chopped

2 cups chicken broth

2 fresh basil sprigs

1 bay leaf

3 tablespoons butter

2 tablespoons all-purpose flour

Salt and pepper to taste

1. Stovetop Pressure Cooker: Place over medium heat. Add oil
   Electrical Pressure Cooker: Select the Sauté function. Add oil.

2. Once hot, add the onion to the cooker and cook for 3 minutes. Add the broth, basil, and bay leaf, seal the cooker, select the High Pressure function and let cook for 10 minutes.

3. Use the natural release method and slowly remove the lid once the pressure has left the cooker. Remove the bay leaf. In a separate bowl, mix the butter and the flour together.

4. Select the Sauté function, add in the flour mixture and let simmer for 5 minutes, stirring constantly. If using a stovetop cooker, place over medium heat.

5. Remove from the cooker and season with salt and pepper to taste.

GO VEGETARIAN!   Replace the chicken broth with Vegetable Stock from page 26.

GO VEGAN!   Replace the chicken broth with Vegetable Stock from page 26 and replace the butter with equal amount coconut oil.

GO GLUTEN-FREE!   Replace the all-purpose flour with corn starch or a gluten-free flour alternative.

GO PALEO!   Replace the all-purpose flour with a grain-free alternative.

HERBED TOMATO SAUCE

MAKES ¾ LITERS ✦ PREP TIME: 20 MINUTES ✦ COOKING TIME: 55 MINUTES

One of my favorite sauces in the book, this sauce goes perfectly with the mini turkey meatballs on page 158 or the Spicy Sausage and Peppers on page 153.

24 oz. can whole tomatoes, peeled

1 tablespoon olive oil

1 tablespoon butter, unsalted

2 cloves garlic, minced

½ teaspoon red pepper flakes

½ tablespoon dried oregano

½ small onion, chopped

½ stem fresh basil

Salt and pepper to taste

1 tablespoon fresh basil leaves

1. Halve the tomatoes horizontally and squeeze out the seeds. Using your hands, crush the tomatoes until pieces no larger than ¼ inch remain.

2. Stovetop Pressure Cooker: Place over medium heat. Add oil and butter. Electrical Pressure Cooker: Select the Sauté function. Add oil and butter.

3. Add the garlic to the mixture once the butter is melted and stir for 3 minutes, or until the garlic has softened. Add the pepper flakes, oregano, onion, and fresh basil, stirring to combine. Add all but 1 cup of the tomatoes, season with salt and pepper, stir, close the lid and set to High Pressure. Let cook for 45 minutes. Place the remaining cup of tomatoes in a sealed container and keep cold.

4. Use the natural release method and slowly remove the lid once the pressure has left the cooker. Remove the onions and the basil from the mixture before adding the remaining tomatoes. Stir well. Add more salt, pepper, or olive oil if desired.

GO VEGAN! Replace butter with equal amount coconut oil.

SWEET AND SPICY BBQ SAUCE

MAKES 5 CUPS ✦ PREP TIME: 10 MINUTES ✦ COOKING TIME: 35 MINUTES

I'm a huge barbecue fan, so much so that this was the first sauce that I added to the book. It's absolutely delicious; the flavors blend in a way that complements any entrée extremely well!

2 tablespoons peanut oil

2 small onions, finely chopped

5 garlic cloves, minced

1 cup tomato purée

1 cup water

½ cup honey

½ cup cider vinegar

1 cup brown sugar

2 tablespoons Dijon mustard

1 teaspoon sea salt

2 teaspoons hot sauce

½ teaspoon cayenne pepper

½ teaspoon black pepper

1. Stovetop Pressure Cooker: Place over medium heat. Add oil. Electrical Pressure Cooker: Select the Sauté function. Add oil.

2. Once hot, place the onion into the pressure cooker and cook for 3 minutes. Add the garlic, tomato purée, water, honey, vinegar, brown sugar, Dijon mustard, sea salt, hot sauce, cayenne pepper, and black pepper and stir well.

3. Once mixed thoroughly, seal the cooker, select the High Pressure function and let cook for 15 minutes.

4. Use the natural release method and slowly remove the lid once the pressure has left the cooker. Stir well and add salt and pepper to taste.

5. Pour the contents of the cooker into a food processor and blend until smooth. Serve immediately.

Tips! – Store in refrigerator for up to 2 weeks or a freezer for 3 months.
– Be sure to check your Dijon mustard brand to make sure that it's gluten-free!

GO VEGAN! Replace honey with equal amount agave nectar.

GO PALEO! Replace brown sugar with ½ cup natural maple syrup and replace the peanut oil with olive oil.

SOUPS & SALADS

In what is perhaps the most versatile section of this book, we look at recipes that are perfect for easing us into our main courses. That said, these recipes can serve a variety of purposes. Looking for a quick snack? Make yourself a serving of the Black Quinoa Salad. In a rush and short on ingredients for some of the main dishes? Up the serving size and have some French Onion Soup for dinner. From timeless classics like Chicken Noodle Soup to the more unique like Creamy Cauliflower Soup, our soups and salads offers a wide variety of options available for all diets.

We start off with salads, all of which are very diet-friendly and easy to make! We mix in a variety of vegetables and ingredients for each recipe, giving everything a unique and identifiable taste. The servings are very easy to adjust here, making it very easy to adjust the amount of people that you're cooking one of these recipes for.

The latter portion of this section contains all of the soup recipes, where we feature some notable staples like Low Carb Chicken Vegetable Soup and French Onion Soup. You may have grown up with variations of some of these recipes, so don't be afraid to stray from what's written if you're seeking nostalgia!

BLACK QUINOA SALAD

MAKES 6 SERVINGS ✦ PREP TIME: 10 MINUTES ✦ COOKING TIME: 10 MINUTES

A recipe accessible to everybody, there really is no better way to eat quinoa than with a little bit of zest.

1 cup black quinoa, rinsed

1 lime, juiced

½ teaspoon salt

1 cup water

1 bunch parsley, chopped

1 mango, diced

2 tomatoes, diced

2 avocados, diced

1 cucumber, seeded and diced

1. Add the quinoa, lime juice, salt, and water to the pressure cooker, seal shut, select the High Pressure function and, if using a stovetop cooker, cook on the lowest heat possible while maintaining high pressure. Let cook for 1½ minutes.

2. Use the natural release method and slowly remove the lid once the pressure has left the cooker. Remove the quinoa from the cooker and place in a separate bowl.

3. Mix in the parsley, mango, tomato, avocado, and cucumber. Season with a dash of salt and serve!

GREEN BEAN AND TOMATO SALAD

MAKES 2 SERVINGS ✦ PREP TIME: 5 MINUTES ✦ COOKING TIME: 8 MINUTES

One of the more minimalist recipes in this entire book, chances are high that you'll have these ingredients laying around on any given day.

1½ tablespoons vegetable oil

½ garlic clove, minced

2 tomatoes, quartered and crushed

1 cup water

½ pound green beans, fresh

½ teaspoon salt

1 teaspoon basil, crushed

1. Stovetop Pressure Cooker: Place over medium heat. Add oil
   Electrical Pressure Cooker: Select the Sauté function. Add oil.

2. Once hot, place the garlic into the pressure cooker and cook for 3 minutes. Add the crushed tomatoes and water to the cooker and mix well.

3. Add the green beans to the steamer basket, season with a dash of salt, and add to the pressure cooker. Seal the cooker, select the High Pressure function and, if using a stovetop cooker, cook on the lowest possible heat while maintaining the high pressure. Let cook for 5 minutes.

4. Use the quick-release method and slowly remove the lid once the pressure has left the cooker. Pour the green beans into the base of the cooker and mix with the tomato sauce. Mix well and remove the green beans from the cooker.

5. Sprinkle the basil and remaining vegetable oil over the beans and serve immediately!

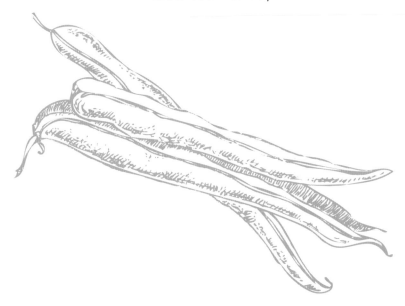

ITALIAN RICE SALAD

MAKES 2 SERVINGS   **PREP TIME: 10 MINUTES**   **COOKING TIME: 10 MINUTES**

Speaking as somebody who attended college next to Little Italy in the Bronx for four years, I can say that this item was a staple on every menu.

1 cup Arborio rice

2 cups water

½ teaspoon salt

1 teaspoon olive oil

1 tomato, diced

1 bunch Basil, chopped

1 mozzarella ball, cubed

2 tablespoons pickles in vinegar

1. Add the rice, water, salt and olive oil into the pressure cooker, seal, select the High Pressure function and, if using a stovetop cooker, cook on as low a heat as possible while maintaining the high pressure. Let cook for 5 minutes.

2. Use the natural release method and slowly remove the lid once the pressure has left the cooker. Pour the rice into a strainer and rinse.

3. Place the rice in a bowl and mix in the remaining ingredients. Serve once mixed well.

GO VEGAN!   Replace the mozzarella ball with ¾ cup canned chickpeas.

KALE AND CARROT SALAD

MAKES 4 SERVINGS ✦ PREP TIME: 5 MINUTES ✦ COOKING TIME: 12 MINUTES

The vinegar garlic combination in the dish is enough to make it a staple in any diet.

2 tablespoons olive oil

5 carrots, peeled and sliced

1 large onion, sliced

7 cloves garlic, minced

2½ cups kale, chopped

1 cup Chicken Bone Broth (page 22)

½ teaspoon salt

½ teaspoon pepper

1 tablespoon cider vinegar

½ teaspoon sugar

1. Stovetop Pressure Cooker: Place over medium heat. Add oil
Electrical Pressure Cooker: Select the Sauté function. Add oil.

2. Once hot, add the carrots, onion and garlic and cook until soft, about 2 minutes. Add in the kale, chicken broth, salt and pepper, seal the cooker, select the High Pressure function and, if using a stovetop cooker, cook on as low a heat as possible while maintaining the high pressure. Let cook for 10 minutes.

3. Use the quick-release method and slowly remove the lid once the pressure has left the cooker. Mix in the cider vinegar and sugar. Remove and serve.

GO VEGAN! Vegetable Stock (page 26) is always a good substitute for Chicken Bone Broth.

SPICY CHICKEN TORTILLA SOUP

MAKES 3 SERVINGS ✦ PREP TIME: 10 MINUTES ✦ COOKING TIME: 20 MINUTES

Spicy Chicken Tortilla Soup is a must-have for anybody who fancies themselves a fan of Spanish cuisine. I love it with shredded cheese, avocado slices, and sour cream.

3 cups chicken broth

¼ cup all-purpose flour

1 tablespoon cayenne pepper

½ tablespoon garlic, minced

1 tablespoon chipotle powder

½ teaspoon salt

1 pound skinless and boneless chicken breast

½ sweet onion, diced

Sour cream

Tortilla chips

Shredded cheese

Avocado, sliced

1. Place the chicken broth, flour, cayenne pepper, garlic, chipotle powder, and salt into a bowl and mix well. Place the mixture, along with the chicken and onion, into the pressure cooker. Seal the cooker, select the High Pressure function, and let cook for 12 minutes.

2. Use the quick-release method and slowly remove the lid once the pressure has left the cooker. Remove the chicken from the mixture, cut to preference, and return to the mixture. Remove the mixture from the pot into a bowl for serving or a container for storage.

3. Serve with whatever toppings you'd like, such as sour cream, tortilla chips, shredded cheese, or avocado slices.

GO VEGETARIAN! Replace the chicken broth with Vegetable Stock from page 26, and replace the chicken with seitan cutlets.

GO VEGAN! Skip the sour cream and cheese or use dairy-free alternatives.

GO GLUTEN-FREE! Replace the all-purpose flour with a gluten-free alternative, and replace the tortilla chips with gluten-free corn chips.

GO PALEO! Replace the all-purpose flour with a grain-free alternative, skip the chips, and pass on the sour cream and cheese. Serve with avocado slices.

CHUNKY POTATO CHEESE SOUP

MAKES 4 SERVINGS ✦ PREP TIME: 5 MINUTES ✦ COOKING TIME: 11 MINUTES

Talk about a guilty pleasure! A soup for all of the stuffed baked potato lovers out there.

1 tablespoon salted butter

12 oz. can chicken broth

½ teaspoon salt

½ teaspoon black pepper

3 cups potatoes, peeled and cubed

1 tablespoon cornstarch

1 tablespoon water

2 oz. cream cheese, cubed

½ cup shredded cheddar cheese

1 cup half and half

3 slices bacon, crumbled

1. Stovetop Pressure Cooker: Place over medium heat. Add butter. Electrical Pressure Cooker: Select the Sauté function. Add butter.

2. Once hot, add the chicken broth, salt, and pepper to the pressure cooker. Stir for 1 minute.

3. Add the diced potatoes to the steamer pot and place in the pressure cooker. Seal the lid, select the High Pressure function and let cook for 5 minutes. After 5 minutes, let sit for another 5 before doing a quick pressure release and removing the steamer basket from the pressure cooker.

4. In a separate dish, dissolve the cornstarch in water. Select the Simmer function on the pressure cooker and add the cornstarch mixture and cheeses to the pot, stirring until the cheese is melted.

5. Add the half and half, bacon, and potatoes to the mixture and let simmer without bringing to a boil. Serve once hot.

 GO VEGETARIAN! Replace chicken broth with equal servings Vegetable Stock from page 26 and hold the bacon.

CREAMY CAULIFLOWER SOUP

MAKES 3 SERVINGS ✦ PREP TIME: 20 MINUTES ✦ COOKING TIME: 20 MINUTES

The Creamy Cauliflower Soup has a lot of the same characteristics that the Chunky Potato Cheese Soup on page 58 does. This, however, has a wider flavor profile and more vegetables.

½ cup salted butter

½ onion, diced

½ cup celery, chopped

½ cup carrot, diced

1 clove garlic, minced

½ head of cauliflower, chopped

½ teaspoon cilantro

2 cups chicken broth

2 tablespoons cornstarch

¾ cup whole milk

½ teaspoon salt

½ teaspoon pepper

½ cup sour cream

½ cup cheddar cheese, grated

4 slices bacon, cooked to a crisp and crumbled

1. Place half of the salted butter to the pressure cooker and select the Sauté function. Once melted, add the onion, celery, carrot, and garlic and let cook for 5 minutes.

2. Add the cauliflower, cilantro, and chicken broth, seal the cooker, and let cook for 3 minutes on Low Pressure.

3. Melt the remaining butter and mix in a bowl with the cornstarch and whole milk. Once creamy, mix in the salt and pepper.

4. Turn the pressure cooker off, let the pressure release naturally for 7 to 10 minutes, then use the quick-release method to unseal the cooker. Select the Simmer function and add in the cornstarch mixture, along with the sour cream and cheddar cheese. Let sit for 5 minutes.

5. Remove the soup and place into a serving bowl or a container, after which sprinkle the crumbled bacon on top.

GO VEGETARIAN! Hold the bacon.

FRENCH ONION SOUP

MAKES 2 CUPS ✦ PREP TIME: 20 MINUTES ✦ COOKING TIME: 40 MINUTES

This classic soup is equally suited as either an appetizer or a light main course with a salad.

¼ cup olive oil

2 tablespoons unsalted butter

1 yellow onion, thinly sliced

¼ teaspoon baking soda

1 teaspoon granulated sugar

Salt and pepper to taste

¼ cup red wine

1 quart chicken or beef stock

1 tablespoon parsley, chopped

1 bay leaf

1 sprig thyme

½ teaspoon cider vinegar

4 slices gluten free Italian bread

¼ cup Parmesan cheese, grated

¾ cup Gruyère cheese, grated

1. Stovetop Pressure Cooker: Place over medium heat. Add oil and butter. Electrical Pressure Cooker: Select the Sauté function. Add oil and butter.

2. Once hot, add the onions and baking soda to the cooker, stir thoroughly, and then add the sugar, salt, and pepper. Cook for 4 minutes, stirring occasionally, until the onions soften. Seal the pressure cooker, select the High Pressure function, and let cook for 18 minutes.

3. Use the natural release method and slowly remove the lid once the pressure has left the cooker and continue cooking until the liquid is gone and the onions are golden brown. Add the red wine and let simmer for 3 minutes. Add the stock, parsley, bay leaf, and thyme to the cooker and let simmer for 13 minutes.

4. Remove the thyme sprig and bay leaf from the mixture. Add the cider vinegar, mix well, and let simmer on low heat.

5. Preheat oven to 450 degrees F. Place slices of Italian bread on the baking sheet and sprinkle with Parmesan cheese. Once heated, bake the bread for 8 minutes.

6. Remove the soup from the pressure cooker, sprinkle Gruyère cheese on top, and serve with baked Italian cheese bread.

 GO VEGETARIAN! Replace the chicken or beef stock with Vegetable Stock (page 26).

BEEF AND VEGETABLE SOUP WITH MUSHROOMS

MAKES 2-4 SERVINGS ✦ PREP TIME: 20 MINUTES ✦ COOKING TIME: 35 MINUTES

A staple, this meal has something to offer any non-vegetarian. Have a distaste for mushrooms? Don't worry, this recipe works just as well without them!

1 teaspoon canola oil

½ large onion, chopped

1 carrot, peeled and sliced

1½ garlic cloves, mashed

1 tablespoon fresh parsley, chopped

2 potatoes, peeled and cubed

1 pound boneless beef, cubed

1 tomato, diced

1 can beef broth

¼ pound fresh mushrooms

1 teaspoon Worcestershire sauce

½ teaspoon salt

½ teaspoon pepper

1. Stovetop Pressure Cooker: Place over medium heat. Add oil
Electrical Pressure Cooker: Select the Sauté function. Add oil.

2. Once hot, add the onion, carrot and beef into the pressure cooker. Cook until the vegetables are caramelized and the beef is browned (8-10 minutes)

3. Add the garlic, parsley, potatoes and tomatoes to the pressure cooker, close the lid, and select the High Heat function. Let cook for 18 minutes.

4. Use the quick-release method to reduce the pressure. Remove the lid and stir in the mushrooms, Worcestershire sauce, salt and pepper. Let the mixture cook in medium heat uncovered for 12 minutes

 **GO VEGAN!** Replace boneless beef with equal amount tofu, and replace the beef broth with Vegetable Stock from page 26.

LOW-CARB CHICKEN VEGETABLE SOUP

MAKES 2 SERVINGS ✦ PREP TIME: 12 MINUTES ✦ COOKING TIME: 32 MINUTES

Because a lot of people grew up with chicken vegetable soup, there are a lot of variations to this recipe floating around out there! Don't hesitate to play with the ingredients if you have a slightly different take on the dish.

1 tablespoon avocado oil

½ pound chicken thighs, boneless and skinless

1 cup radishes, diced

1 cup carrots, diced

½ cup green onion, chopped

3 cups chicken stock

½ teaspoon oregano

½ teaspoon salt

¼ teaspoon pepper

1. Stovetop Pressure Cooker: Place over medium heat. Add oil
Electrical Pressure Cooker: Select the Sauté function. Add oil.

2. Once the instant pot is hot, add chicken and cook for 10 minutes. Remove the chicken from the pot and shred using two forks.

3. Return the chicken, along with the radishes, carrots, and onions to the pot and cook for 3 minutes. Add the stock, oregano, salt, and pepper to the pot, seal, select the Soup setting and let cook for 20 minutes.

4. Use the natural release method and slowly remove the lid once the pressure has left the cooker.

GO VEGAN! Replace the chicken with seitan and the chicken stock with Vegetable Stock found on page 26.

EGG ROLL SOUP

MAKES 2-4 SERVINGS ✦ PREP TIME: 5 MINUTES ✦ COOKING TIME: 40 MINUTES

This recipe is, in my opinion, one of the more unique recipes here! If I have the time to make it, I'm good for this meal at least once a week.

2 tablespoons olive oil

2 pounds ground pork

2 large red onions, diced

6 cups chicken broth

6 carrots, shredded

2 teaspoons onion powder

2 teaspoons garlic, minced

2 teaspoons ginger, ground

Salt to taste

1. Stovetop Pressure Cooker: Place over medium heat. Add oil
Electrical Pressure Cooker: Select the Sauté function. Add oil.

2. When hot, add the ground pork. Brown on each side for about 5 minutes before removing from cooker. Add the onions, let cook for 3 minutes, then return the pork, along with all remaining ingredients, to the cooker. Seal shut, select the High Pressure function, and let cook for 30 minutes.

3. Use the quick-release method and slowly remove the lid once the pressure has left the cooker. Remove the soup and serve.

STEWS

The stews in this book are heavy and, except in the case of the big eaters out there, can likely serve as their own meal altogether! Although most of these dishes are beef or seafood based, their bold flavors are largely due to the vegetables and spices included the meat. Most of these dishes don't take too long to prepare, though they do fall into the 15- to 20-minute range, so leave yourself some time to prepare.

My focus when creating this section of the book was variety. I wanted to include dishes that featured different meats and spices that came from all corners of the world. Northeasterners like myself have been exposed to dishes like New England Clam Chowder before, but I had not experienced, for example, the flavors of the Greek Zesty Fish Stew prior to moving to Astoria, a section of New York City that is home to a large Greek population. My end goal was to introduce some new flavors while playing to nostalgia with some old ones!

BEEF BOURGUIGNON

MAKES 3 SERVINGS ✦ PREP TIME: 30 MINUTES ✦ COOKING TIME: 17 MINUTES

A delicious meaty dish for anybody who enjoys red meat.

1 tablespoon olive oil

2 slices bacon, diced

¾ pound chuck roast beef, boneless and cubed

2 carrots, peeled and chopped

½ teaspoon salt

¼ teaspoon basil, crushed

1⅓ cup mushrooms, quartered

1 clove garlic, minced

⅓ cup beef broth

⅓ cup red wine

1 tablespoon tomato paste

1 tablespoon flour

2 tablespoons water

1. Stovetop Pressure Cooker: Place over medium heat. Add oil Electrical Pressure Cooker: Select the Sauté function. Add oil.

2. Once hot, place the bacon in the pressure cooker and cook for 2 to 3 minutes. Once browned, add the beef, carrots, salt, basil, mushrooms, garlic, broth, wine, and tomato paste. Seal the cover, select the High Pressure function and, if using a stovetop cooker, cook on as low a heat as possible while maintaining the pressure. Let cook for 12 minutes.

3. Use the natural release method and slowly remove the lid once the pressure has left the cooker.

4. Whisk the flour and water together in a separate bowl and, when well combined, add to the pressure cooker. Stir well before returning the cooker to medium heat while leaving uncovered. Stir frequently and cook until 2 minutes after the stew has thickened. Let cool for 2 minutes before serving.

GO GLUTEN-FREE! Replace the flour with a gluten-free alternative.

GO PALEO! Replace the flour with a grain-less alternative.

CIOPPINO

MAKES 2-3 SERVINGS • **PREP TIME: 5 MINUTES** • **COOKING TIME: 15 MINUTES**

This delicious seafood stew is made with shrimp and white fish.

1½ tablespoons olive oil

½ large onion, diced

1 celery stalk, chopped

2 cloves garlic, minced

1 bay leaf

¼ cup parsley, chopped

1½ tablespoons basil, chopped

½ teaspoon red pepper flakes

½ teaspoon dried oregano

1 cup red wine

⅔ can (28-oz) diced tomatoes, with juice

1 bottle (8-oz) clam juice

½ pound large shrimp, uncooked and peeled

½-pound cod fillets (or other white fish), washed and cut into 1-inch pieces

1. Stovetop Pressure Cooker: Place over medium heat. Add oil
Electrical Pressure Cooker: Select the Sauté function. Add oil.

2. Once hot, add the onion to the pressure cooker and cook for 3 minutes. Add the celery, garlic, bay leaf, parsley, basil, red pepper flakes, oregano, and red wine. Stir until the red wine has reduced to half.

3. Add the tomatoes and clam juice to the cooker and bring to a simmer. Season with salt and pepper to taste.

4. Add the shrimp to the cooker, followed by the cod fillets. Seal, select the High Pressure function and, if using a stovetop cooker, cook on as low a heat as possible while maintaining the high pressure. Let cook for 4 minutes.

5. Use the natural release method and slowly remove the lid once the pressure has left the cooker. Stir and season with salt and pepper to taste before serving.

NEW ENGLAND CLAM CHOWDER

MAKES 2 SERVINGS ✦ PREP TIME: 7 MINUTES ✦ COOKING TIME: 14 MINUTES

This is, not surprisingly, my favorite dish to come out of the New England area. The creamy consistency combined with the whole-belly clams makes everything about it delicious. Oh, and don't forget your oyster crackers!

6 strips bacon, diced

2 cups onion, chopped

4 medium potatoes, cubed

2 teaspoons salt

½ teaspoon white pepper

4 cups clam juice

½ teaspoon red pepper flakes

½ teaspoon basil

2 cups whole milk

2 cups half and half

2 tablespoons salted butter

2 tablespoons flour

2 dozen fresh clams

Oyster crackers (optional)

1. Add the bacon to the pressure cooker and cook using low heat. Once sizzling, add the onions and let cook until they've softened.

2. Next, add the potatoes, salt, pepper, clam juice, red pepper flakes and basil into the pressure cooker, and then secure the lid and select the High Pressure function. Let cook for 7 minutes.

3. Use the natural release method and slowly remove the lid once the pressure has left the cooker. Add the milk, half and half, butter, flour, and clams to the mixture and stir well. Let simmer over medium heat for 7 minutes.

4. Serve with oyster crackers and enjoy!

Make your own clam juice! – Place your fresh clams in the steamer basket of the pressure cooker, add 1 cup of water, and let cook on low heat and high pressure for 7 minutes. Now you have clam meat that's ready to serve and plenty of clam juice at the bottom of the cooker!

GO GLUTEN-FREE! Replace the flour with equal servings gluten-free alternative.

SPICY MEXICAN BEEF STEW

MAKES 2-4 SERVINGS ✦ PREP TIME: 5 MINUTES ✦ COOKING TIME: 42 MINUTES

The perfect dish for somebody looking to get a little kick out of their stew. Add as much or as little chili and chipotle powder as you want to control how much heat this dish serves out.

1 tablespoon salted butter

½ onion, diced

1-pound chuck roast beef

1 teaspoon salt

1 teaspoon chili powder

1 teaspoon chipotle powder

1 teaspoon dried oregano

¼ teaspoon pepper

½ cup beef broth

7 ounces fire-roasted tomatoes

3 ounces green chilies, diced

Cheddar cheese, shredded

Sour cream

Avocado, sliced

Cilantro

1. Stovetop Pressure Cooker: Place over medium heat. Add butter. Electrical Pressure Cooker: Select the Sauté function. Add butter.

2. Once heated, add the onions and cook until golden brown, about 3 minutes.

3. Season the beef with salt, chili and chipotle powders, dried oregano and pepper before adding to the pressure cooker. Sear meat for 3 minutes per side.

4. Add the broth, tomatoes and chilies to the cooker, seal the cover, and select the High Pressure function. Cook on as low a heat as possible while maintaining the high pressure for 30 minutes.

5. Use a quick pressure release and slowly remove the cover once the valve has dropped. Serve with preferred amounts of cheddar cheese, sour cream, avocado, and cilantro.

 GO VEGETARIAN! Replace the beef with tofu and the beef broth with the Vegetable Stock found on page 26.

VEGETABLE CHILI

MAKES 4 SERVINGS ✦ PREP TIME: 5 MINUTES ✦ COOKING TIME: 6 MINUTES

You don't have to be a vegetarian to enjoy this dish! The scallions really bring everything together here, as they go great with the beans and the corn. And the best part? It only takes 6 minutes to cook!

1 tablespoon olive oil

2 garlic cloves, minced

1 green pepper, diced

10 scallions, chopped

1 tablespoon chili powder

2 teaspoons cumin, ground

½ teaspoon salt

½ teaspoon pepper

2 cans black beans, rinsed and drained

1 cup pinto beans, soaked

1 cup red kidney beans, soaked

2 tomatoes, diced

1 cup corn

2 cups vegetable stock

Shredded cheddar cheese, sour cream, and chives as topping options

1. Stovetop Pressure Cooker: Place over medium heat. Add oil. Electrical Pressure Cooker: Select the Sauté function. Add oil.

2. Once hot, add garlic, green pepper, and scallions. Let cook for 3 minutes, or until the vegetables soften. Add the chili powder, cumin, salt, and pepper and stir for another minute.

3. Add the beans, tomatoes, corn, and vegetable stock, seal the lid, select the High Pressure function, and let cook for 3 minutes.

4. Use a quick-release method and slowly remove the lid once the valve has dropped. Stir well. Top with shredded cheddar cheese, sour cream, or chives, as desired, and salt and pepper to taste.

Tip! – If the chili isn't as thick as desired, simply sauté on high heat for 3 to 5 minutes For some added flavor, add a few pinches of shredded cheddar cheese to the chili!

GO PALEO! Hold the cheese and sour cream.

ZESTY GREEK FISH STEW

MAKES 4 SERVINGS ✦ PREP TIME: 5 MINUTES ✦ COOKING TIME: 5 MINUTES

Who doesn't love their seafood with a little bit of zest? Much like the Black Quinoa Salad on page 49, I'm a believer that white fish is infinitely better with a little bit of lemon juice.

3 tablespoons vegetable oil

1 onion, diced

2 garlic cloves, minced

¼ cup fresh parsley, chopped

2 tablespoons dried oregano

2 cups seafood stock

¾ cup dried white wine

5 lemons, juiced

1 zucchini, ends removed and thinly sliced

1½ pounds white fish fillet, washed and cubed

1 tablespoon cornstarch

1 bay leaf

Salt and pepper to taste

1. Stovetop Pressure Cooker: Place over medium heat. Add oil. Electrical Pressure Cooker: Select the Sauté function. Add oil.

2. Once heated, add the onion and garlic to the pressure cooker and cook for 3 minutes.

3. Add the parsley, oregano, seafood stock, white wine, lemon juice, zucchini, fish fillets, and cornstarch. Mix well before adding the bay leaf. Seal, select the Low Pressure function, and let cook for 2 minutes.

4. Use the natural release method and slowly remove the lid once the valve has dropped. Remove the bay leaf, stir, and season with salt and pepper to taste before serving.

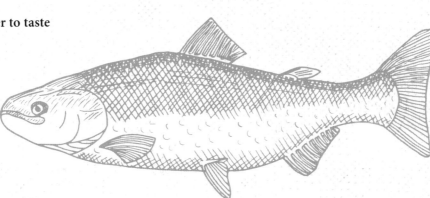

KIDNEY BEAN CURRY

MAKES 4 SERVINGS ✦ PREP TIME: 10 MINUTES ✦ COOKING TIME: 1 HOUR

A very diet-friendly meal, this bean dish packs a flavorful kick that anybody can enjoy. Never had Kidney Bean Curry? Trek outside of your comfort zone! You'll be glad that you did.

½ yellow onion, chopped

2 cloves garlic, minced

½ piece fresh ginger root, chopped

1 tablespoon vegetable oil

1 dried red chile pepper, broken up

3 whole cloves

1 teaspoon coriander seeds

½ teaspoon turmeric, ground

½ teaspoon chipotle powder

½ teaspoon coriander, ground

1 tomato, diced

1 cup dried red kidney beans, soaked overnight

2 cups water

½ teaspoon sugar

½ teaspoon salt

1 teaspoon garam masala

½ teaspoon red pepper flakes

2 tablespoons cilantro leaves, chopped

1. Grind together the onion, garlic, and ginger using a mortar and pestle. Crush and grind until contents are mixed well and have the consistency of a paste.

2. Stovetop Pressure Cooker: Place over medium heat. Add oil.
   Electrical Pressure Cooker: Select the Sauté function. Add oil.

3. Once hot, add the red chile pepper, whole cloves and coriander seeds. Cook for about 90 seconds before adding the garlic paste to the cooker. Stir well. Add the turmeric, chipotle, coriander, and tomatoes to the cooker. Stir until the tomatoes are soft.

4. Add the beans, water, sugar, and salt to the cooker, seal, select the High Pressure function, and cook for about 42 minutes. Lower the heat and let simmer for another 8 minutes.

5. Use the natural release method and slowly remove the lid once the valve drops. Stir the garam masala, red pepper flakes, and cilantro leaves into the mixture before serving.

APPETIZERS

Often we find ourselves indulging on heavy appetizers that leave us no room for our main course. While chowing down on chicken wings and sliders always makes for a good time, their daily consumption isn't exactly practical. This section leans more towards the lighter side of things, with recipes like Eggplant and Roasted Red Pepper Dip and Sweet and Sour Carrots and Parsnips that are perfect for sharing with friends before a meal. These recipes are especially useful for anybody who loves to host parties or get-togethers; they're easy to share and usually make for a quick cleanup.

Dips are featured pretty heavily in this section. Easy to make and easier to store, these dishes are inviting, practical, and are difficult to mess up! I've spanned the health spectrum here; from the Chipotle Chickpea Hummus to the Bean and Cheese Queso Dip, some of these dishes are healthier than others. That said, anything can be enjoyed in moderation, and these dips are no exception.

You'll also find dishes like Marinated Mushrooms and Edamame with Garlic and Butter that, while relatively light, are great for snacking on and enjoying before a big meal. They're also pretty healthy as well, inviting that guiltless pleasure that's so hard to come by when eating flavorful food!

BEAN AND CHEESE QUESO DIP

MAKES 3-4 SERVINGS ✦ PREP TIME: 5 MINUTES ✦ COOKING TIME: 20 MINUTES

I'll admit that I like cheese queso dip a little bit too much… to the point where I've thought to myself, more than a few times, "I have to stop eating this queso!" From personal experience, this recipe makes the world's best queso, so good that it's almost addictive!

4 cups refried beans

1¼ cup green chile, chopped

1¼ cup tomatoes, diced

2 teaspoons basil

1 teaspoon chili powder

¼ teaspoon salt

¼ teaspoon pepper

4 cans Progresso's three-cheese cooking sauce

½ cup cilantro, chopped

1. Place the refried beans, chile, tomatoes, basil, chili powder, salt, pepper, and cheese sauce into the pressure cooker and stir well. Seal the cooker, select the Low Pressure function, and let cook for 2 hours and 20 minutes.

2. Use the natural release method and slowly remove the lid once the pressure has left the cooker. Mix in the cilantro, remove from the cooker, and serve.

SWEET AND SOUR CARROTS AND PARSNIPS

MAKES 2 SERVINGS ✦ PREP TIME: 3 MINUTES ✦ COOKING TIME: 3 MINUTES

The carrots and parsnips complement each other as well as the vinegar and maple syrup do in this recipe. This app also makes for a delicious snack when you're looking for something small and quick.

2 carrots, peeled and sliced

¾ pound parsnips, peeled and sliced

¼ cup Vegetable Stock (store-bought or from page 26)

2 tablespoons balsamic vinegar

3 tablespoons organic maple syrup

Salt and pepper to taste

1. Place the carrots, parsnips, vegetable stock, and vinegar in the pressure cooker, seal shut, select the High Pressure function, and then let cook for 3 minutes.

2. Use the quick-release method and slowly remove the lid once the pressure has left the cooker. Mix in the maple syrup. Season with salt and pepper to taste before serving.

Tip! – For some added flavor, sear with a thin coating of oil in a pan over medium-high heat for several minutes!

SPICY SHRIMP SCAMPI

MAKES 4 SERVINGS ✦ PREP TIME: 15 MINUTES ✦ COOKING TIME: 10 MINUTES

A spicy twist on a classic dish, this appetizer is packed with flavors that come together perfectly.

¼ cup olive oil

3 garlic cloves, minced

½ tablespoon paprika

1 pound extra-large shrimp, peeled and deveined

¼ cup dried white wine

1½ tablespoons fresh parsley, chopped

Salt and pepper to taste

Lemon wedges

1. Add the olive oil, garlic, paprika, shrimp, wine, and parsley in the pressure cooker and mix well. Seal shut, select the High Pressure function, and let cook for 10 minutes.

2. Use the natural release method and slowly remove the lid once the pressure has left the cooker. Season to taste with salt, pepper, and lemon before serving.

BUTTERNUT SQUASH RISOTTO

MAKES 3 SERVINGS ✦ PREP TIME: 10 MINUTES ✦ COOKING TIME: 15 MINUTES

This recipe is super-easy to make and yields a delicious plate suitable to any pallet.

1 tablespoon unsalted butter

1½ tablespoons rosemary, chopped

1 cup butternut squash, peeled and cubed

1 clove garlic, minced

½ small onion, chopped

½ teaspoon salt

1 cup chicken stock

¾ cup Arborio rice

1 cup water

½ cup Parmesan cheese, grated

Salt and pepper to taste

1. Stovetop Pressure Cooker: Place over medium heat. Add butter. Electrical Pressure Cooker: Select the Sauté function. Add butter.

2. Once heated, add the rosemary and cook for 90 seconds.

3. Mix in the onions and let cook for 5 minutes. Add the squash, garlic, onion, and salt to the mixture and let cook for another 5 minutes.

4. Mix in the chicken stock, rice, and water, seal the cooker, select the High Pressure function, and lower the heat once that pressure is achieved while still maintaining that pressure. Let cook for 5 minutes.

5. Use the quick-release method to release the pressure and let sit for several minutes. Unseal the cooker, mix in the cheese, and season as desired.

GO VEGETARIAN! Replace the chicken stock with Vegetable Stock (store-bought or from page 26).

CHIPOTLE CHICKPEA HUMMUS

MAKES 4 SERVINGS ◆ PREP TIME: 10 MINUTES ◆ COOKING TIME: 15-18 MINUTES

A favorite of mine, I first tried this dish in northern Michigan and have been obsessed with it ever since. It's a perfect snack with tortilla chips, pita bread, or carrots.

½ cup chickpeas

3 cups water

2 garlic cloves, crushed

1 tablespoon sesame oil

½ lemon

1 tablespoon cumin, powdered

Salt to taste

Extra virgin olive oil

1 tablespoon Parsley leaves

Chipotle powder

1. Rinse the chickpeas and, along with the water and one garlic clove, add to the pressure cooker. Cover, select High Pressure, and cook for 20 minutes.

2. After 20 minutes, open the pressure cooker using the natural release method and let sit for 10 minutes. Drain the chickpeas while reserving the cooking liquid, setting aside for later use. Allow the chickpeas to cool for several minutes.

3. Add the chickpeas, ½ of the cooking liquid, sesame oil, lemon juice, and remaining crushed garlic clove to a food processor and purée. If the mixture isn't creamy enough, slowly add remaining cooking liquid until the right consistency is achieved. Add salt to taste and purée again.

4. Empty the food processor into a container. Create a center groove and add olive oil. Sprinkle the hummus with parsley and chipotle powder before serving.

EDAMAME WITH GARLIC AND BUTTER

MAKES 4 SERVINGS | **PREP TIME: 5 MINUTES** | **COOKING TIME: 4 MINUTES**

Perhaps the simplest recipe in this entire book, this dish is flavorful, light, and incredibly easy to make.

1 cup water

2 cups edamame, with pods

1 teaspoon salted butter, melted

2 garlic cloves, minced

1 tablespoon soy sauce

Salt to taste

1. Add the water and edamame in the pressure cooker's steamer basket, seal shut, select the Steam and High Pressure functions, and let cook for 4 minutes.

2. While the edamame is cooking, mix together the butter, garlic and soy sauce in a medium bowl. Set aside until the edamame is done.

3. Use the quick-release method and slowly remove the lid once the valve has dropped. Empty the steamer basket into the bowl and mix together the edamame and the sauce. Add salt to taste before serving.

GO VEGAN! Replace the salted butter with canola oil.

EGGPLANT AND ROASTED RED PEPPER DIP

MAKES 4 SERVINGS ✦ PREP TIME: 10 MINUTES ✦ COOKING TIME: 20 MINUTES

I started working eggplant into my diet during my brief stint as a vegetarian, though now I try to work it in wherever possible! Eggplant goes great with this roasted red pepper dip, a diet-friendly snack that works for any occasion.

2 tablespoons olive oil

2 cloves garlic, minced

1 large eggplant, peeled and chunked

½ cup water

½ teaspoon salt

½ cup roasted red peppers, diced

2 tablespoons lemon juice

½ tablespoon fresh basil

½ teaspoon ground cumin

Freshly ground pepper

Pita chips or toast

1. Stovetop Pressure Cooker: Place over medium heat. Add 1 tablespoon oil. Electrical Pressure Cooker: Select the Sauté function. Add 1 tablespoon oil.

2. Once heated, add the garlic and eggplant, browning the eggplant on each side for four minutes. Add the water and salt, seal, select the High Pressure function, and then let cook for 3 minutes.

3. Use the quick-release method and slowly remove the cover once the valve falls. Stir in the red peppers and let sit for 7 minutes.

4. Drain out any cooking liquid. Add 1 tablespoon oil, lemon juice, basil, cumin, and pepper. Stir until smooth. Serve with pita chips or toast.

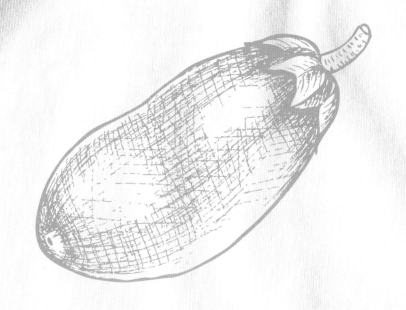

SPINACH ARTICHOKE DIP

MAKES 6 SERVINGS ✦ PREP TIME: 5 MINUTES ✦ COOKING TIME: 12 MINUTES

Another personal favorite of mine (I love my dips), this goes very well with baked pita chips.

¾ cup spinach, chopped

¾ cup artichoke hearts, chopped

½ cup mayonnaise

½ cup provolone cheese, shredded

½ cup Parmesan cheese, shredded

½ cup cream cheese

¼ cup sour cream

1 teaspoon garlic, minced

⅛ teaspoon ground black pepper

2 cups water

1. Mix all ingredients, minus the water, in a small baking dish that will fit inside of your pressure cooker. Once mixed well, cover the dish tightly in foil.

2. Place the water into the pressure cooker, followed by the baking dish. Seal the cover, select the High Pressure function, and let cook for 12 minutes.

3. Use the quick-release method and carefully remove the lid once the valve has dropped. Remove the baking dish and check to make sure that the cheese has melted before serving.

MARINATED MUSHROOMS

SERVES 2 TO 3 ✦ PREP TIME: 5 MINUTES ✦ COOKING TIME: 5 MINUTES

A last-second addition to the book, these mushrooms are delicious by themselves and can be worked into most recipes calling for crimini mushrooms.

½ pound whole crimini mushrooms, trimmed

½ cup white vinegar

½ cup water

½ teaspoon basil

½ teaspoon oregano

½ teaspoon thyme

6 cloves garlic, minced

½ teaspoon salt

1. Add all of the ingredients to the pressure cooker, seal shut, select the High Pressure function, and let cook for 5 minutes.

2. Use the natural release method and slowly remove the lid once the pressure has left the cooker. Transfer to a dish for serving or to a jar for up to a week of refrigeration.

STUFFED BELL PEPPERS

MAKES 2 SERVINGS ✦ PREP TIME: 5 MINUTES ✦ COOKING TIME: 12 MINUTES

This was a staple in my house growing up, though I was always hesitant to try it. Now I can't get enough! When shared these make the perfect appetizers, while making one or two for yourself serves as an excellent meal in and of itself. Don't like green bell peppers? Any color works! Tailor this recipe to your preference.

1 tablespoon olive oil

4 slices bacon, cut into ½-inch pieces

¼ pound ground beef

2 tablespoons onion, chopped

½ teaspoon salt

½ teaspoon pepper

⅛ teaspoon poultry seasoning

½ cup rice, cooked

1 egg, beaten

2 green bell peppers, tops removed, cored and deseeded

1 cup water

1. Add olive oil and bacon to the pressure cooker and cook over medium heat until crispy, about 5 minutes. Remove bacon and add the ground beef and onion, cooking until the beef is browned and the onion is softened and slightly golden brown.

2. Remove the beef and onions from the pressure cooker and place in a mixing bowl. Add the bacon pieces, salt, pepper, poultry seasoning, rice, and egg to the bowl and mix well.

3. Fill each pepper with the meat mixture. Add the cup of water to the pressure cooker, along with the stuffed peppers on the rack. Seal the pressure cooker, select the High Pressure function, and let cook for 12 minutes.

4. Use the natural release method and slowly remove the lid once the valve has dropped.

STUFFED CABBAGE ROLLS WITH BROWN RICE

MAKES 6 SERVINGS ✦ PREP TIME: 10 MINUTES ✦ COOKING TIME: 40 MINUTES

I wasn't familiar with this dish until very recently, which was when I realized that I had been missing out. For those not familiar, this recipe should be a must try.

½ head cabbage

½ teaspoon butter

½ cup onion, chopped

1½ cloves garlic, minced

1 teaspoon beef broth

2 tablespoons white vinegar

1 tablespoon Worcestershire sauce

½ teaspoon black pepper, crushed

4 tomatoes, diced

½ can tomato sauce

¼ teaspoon dried oregano leaves

1 egg, beaten

½ cup onion, chopped

2 cloves garlic, minced

½ teaspoon salt

½ teaspoon pepper

½ cup brown rice, cooked

¾ pound ground beef

½ cup Parmesan cheese, grated

1. Bring water to a boil over high heat and place cabbage in the pot, core side down. Cover and let cook for 10 minutes.

2. Begin removing the softened outer layers of the cabbages and then set them aside to cool. After another 10 minutes of cooking, the remaining leaves should be too small to roll. Remove what's left, chop it up, and set it aside.

3. Place the butter and the onion in a sauce pan and cook over medium heat. Once the onions begin to look caramelized, which should only take several minutes, add the garlic, broth, vinegar, Worcestershire sauce, black pepper, tomatoes, tomato sauce, oregano, and cabbage leaves that were too small to roll. Stir well and remove from heat.

4. In a separate bowl, mix together the egg, onion, garlic, salt, pepper, cooked rice, and ground beef. Mix well.

5. On a flat surface, lay out the cooked cabbage leaves so that the stem end is closest to you. Place 3 tablespoons of the ground beef mixture at the bottom of the leaf, fold the sides in and roll toward the top. Repeat until there is no more filling left.

6. Add one cup of water to the pressure cooker and add the cabbage rolls to the rack. Pour half of the sauce over the rolls, making sure to cover all sides. Close the lid, select the High Pressure function, and let cook for 20 minutes.

7. Let sit for 10 minutes before using the Quick-Release Pressure function to release the pressure. Remove the cover and place the rolls on a serving dish. Pour the remaining sauce and the grated cheese over the rolls before serving.

WHITE BEAN DIP

MAKES 4 CUPS   **PREP TIME: 5 MINUTES**   **COOKING TIME: 30 MINUTES**

Here we have yet another dip. This one is very diet-friendly, very healthy, and goes well with baked pita chips.

1½ cups dried white beans, rinsed

4 cups water

4 garlic cloves, minced

⅔ cup olive oil

½ teaspoon salt

½ teaspoon pepper

2 teaspoons cumin, ground

2 teaspoons chili powder

1 teaspoon red pepper flakes

½ lemon, juiced

½ teaspoon rosemary, chopped

Place the beans, water, garlic, olive oil, salt, pepper, cumin, chili powder, and red pepper flakes into the pressure cooker. Seal shut, select the High Pressure function, and let cook for 30 minutes.

Use the natural release method and slowly remove the lid once the valve has dropped. Pour the contents of the cooker through a strainer into a container, separating the beans from the cooking liquid.

Place the beans in a food processor and blend until smooth. If the mixture is too thick, add 1 tablespoon of the cooking liquid at a time until desired consistency is achieved. The cooking liquid can now be discarded.

Season the dip with salt and pepper to taste before serving.

CHICKEN ENCHILADAS

MAKES 3-4 SERVINGS ✦ PREP TIME: 20 MINUTES ✦ COOKING TIME: 40 MINUTES

You'd do just as well to serve this as an entrée, though I find that I enjoy this dish most in smaller servings.

1 pound chicken thighs, boneless and skinless

½ jalapeño pepper, sliced

2 plum tomatoes, diced

½ onion, sliced

2 cloves garlic, minced

½ teaspoon ground cumin seed

1 teaspoon dried oregano

¼ cup chicken stock

½ teaspoon salt

½ teaspoon pepper

½ lime, juiced

½ tablespoon soy sauce

¼ cup cheddar cheese, shredded

2 tablespoons cotija cheese, crumbled

2 tablespoons fresh cilantro, chopped

2 fresh corn tortillas

1. Add chicken, jalapeños, tomatoes, onion, garlic, cumin, oregano, stock, salt, and pepper to the pressure cooker and stir until mixed well. Seal the pressure cooker, select the High Pressure function, and let cook for 17 minutes.

2. Use the quick-release method and slowly remove the lid once the valve goes down. Remove the chicken from the mixture and set aside to cool.

3. Place the remaining contents of the pressure cooker into a blender and, after adding the lime juice and soy sauce, blend until smooth.

4. Shred the chicken with two forks and, when done, divide the chicken in half. Place one half on one side of a corn tortilla, pour sauce from the blender over top of chicken and season with cheeses, cilantro, salt and pepper. Fold and serve.

GO VEGETARIAN!   Remove the chicken from the recipe and replace the chicken stock with Vegetable Stock (store-bought or from page 26).

GO GLUTEN FREE!   Replace the corn tortillas with a gluten-free alternative.

MAIN DISHES

Here we are! We've reached the meat of the book;
it is here that you will find your classic entrée-style
dishes that invite your imagination and creativity.
These recipes, while structured, offer us more room
to play around without compromising the recipe itself.
We have the flexibility to really make the dish our own.
Switch out spices, mix and match the vegetables,
change up the meat; really allow yourself to dig in
and explore the recipes. Of course, they yield quite
a delicious final product, so don't worry about missing
out if you don't feel comfortable changing anything up!

We start with the poultry dishes, which are varied and
unique from one another. You'll find a recipe for Cacciatore
Chicken followed by a recipe for Chicken and Asparagus
in this section; both poultry based but entirely different
dishes all together. A few Asian dishes are worked in
as well, allowing us to get a taste of Chinese and Indian
cuisines as we make our way through the section.

You'll then find recipes for beef, pork, and lamb following
the poultry. We lean on the staples here, featuring recipes

CACCIATORE CHICKEN

MAKES 4-6 SERVINGS ✦ PREP TIME: 20 MINUTES ✦ COOKING TIME: 10 MINUTES

Serve on top of spaghetti or with a side of fennel to get the most out of the dish.

2 tablespoons olive oil

2 chicken breasts, halved, boneless and skinned

2 onions, halved and sliced

4 garlic cloves, minced

1 pound cremini mushrooms, trimmed and sliced

1 can diced tomatoes, undrained

½ cup dry white wine

½ teaspoon thyme, dried

1 teaspoon sage, dried

1 teaspoon rosemary, dried

Salt and pepper to taste

1. Stovetop Pressure Cooker: Place over medium heat. Add 1 tablespoon oil. Electrical Pressure Cooker: Select the Sauté function. Add 1 tablespoon oil.

2. Once heated, add half of the chicken breast and then brown on both sides for 3 minutes each. Once browned, remove and repeat with the other half of chicken breast.

3. Add 1 tablespoon olive oil and onion and cook for 3 minutes. Add the garlic and cook for another minute, stirring periodically. Add the mushrooms, tomatoes, wine, thyme, sage and rosemary. Mix well.

4. Place the rack into the cooker and add the chicken. Seal, select High Pressure, and let cook for 7 minutes.

5. Use the natural release method and slowly remove the lid once the pressure has left the cooker. Remove the chicken, cover with the remaining contents of the cooker, and season with salt and pepper to taste before serving.

GO VEGAN! Replace the chicken breasts with equal servings seitan.

CHICKEN AND ASPARAGUS

MAKES 2-3 SERVINGS ✦ PREP TIME: 5 MINUTES ✦ COOKING TIME: 35 MINUTES

This dish is a staple in my diet. I prefer my asparagus seasoned with plenty of salt and doused with olive oil, though I would suggest taking a slightly healthier approach.

1 tablespoon olive oil

3 chicken thighs, rinsed with skin removed

1 cup chicken stock

1½ tablespoons fresh cilantro, chopped

½ tablespoon fresh basil

½ tablespoon fresh rosemary, chopped

½ tablespoon fresh tarragon

½ bay leaf

1 cloves garlic, minced

4 bottomless stalks asparagus, cut into ½-inch pieces

Salt and pepper to taste

1. Stovetop Pressure Cooker: Place over medium heat. Add oil. Electric Pressure Cooker: Select the Sauté function. Add oil.

2. Once heated, place the chicken pieces in the cooker and cook until each side is browned, about 3 minutes each side. Remove and set aside.

3. Add stock, cilantro, basil, rosemary, tarragon, bay leaf, garlic, and asparagus to the cooker and stir well. Place the chicken pieces into the cooker, close the lid, Select the High Pressure function, and then let cook for 6 minutes.

4. Use the natural release method and slowly remove the lid once the pressure has left the cooker. Remove bay leaf. Season to taste before serving.

Tip! – For added flavor, sear the chicken with a thin coating of oil in a pan over medium-high heat for several minutes on each side!

GO VEGAN! Replace the chicken thighs with equal servings seitan and the chicken stock with equal amount Vegetable Stock (store-bought or from page 26).

BEER-SOAKED CHICKEN

MAKES 2 SERVINGS ✦ PREP TIME: 10 MINUTES ✦ COOKING TIME: 25 MINUTES

The dark beer adds some great flavor without overpowering the dish, while the cilantro and rosemary complete what is a great-tasting meal!

2 tablespoons unsalted butter, melted

½ red onion, peeled and cubed

¼ cup all-purpose flour

½ whole chicken, skinned and cut to preference

Bottle of dark beer

1 tablespoon cilantro, minced

1 tablespoon rosemary, minced

Salt and pepper to taste

1. Stovetop Pressure Cooker: Place over medium heat. Add butter. Electric Pressure Cooker: Select the Sauté function. Add butter.

2. Once heated, place the cubed onions in the pressure cooker and let cook for 2 minutes until the onions are soft and translucent, stirring occasionally. Remove and set aside.

3. Coat the chicken pieces in the all-purpose flour, covering completely before adding each piece to the cooker. On medium heat, brown each piece of chicken for 3 to 5 minutes per side. Remove each piece once browned and set aside.

4. Pour the bottle of beer into the pressure cooker, bring to a boil, then lower heat and let simmer. Place the chicken back in the cooker, close the lid, and select the High Heat function. Reduce the heat once high pressure is achieved and let cook for 10 minutes.

5. Use the quick-release method and slowly remove the lid once the pressure has left the cooker. Sprinkle cilantro, rosemary, salt, and pepper over the chicken.

GO GLUTEN-FREE! Check to make sure that the dark beer you're using is gluten-free. If not, find a gluten-free alternative; there are plenty of them out there. And then replace the flour with a gluten-free alternative, as well.

CHICKEN MARSALA

MAKES 4 SERVINGS ✦ PREP TIME: 10 MINUTES ✦ COOKING TIME: 20 MINUTES

Serve this with Creamy Mashed Potatoes with Sour Cream (page 187) or Sweet and Sour Carrots and Parsnips (page 94).

2 tablespoons olive oil

2 pounds chicken breasts, boneless and skinless

1 yellow onion, diced

4 garlic cloves, minced

¾ cup Marsala wine

½ cup fresh parsley, chopped

¼ cup chicken stock

Salt and pepper to taste

1. Stovetop Pressure Cooker: Place over medium heat. Add 1 tablespoon oil. Electric Pressure Cooker: Select the Sauté function. Add 1 tablespoon oil.

2. Once heated, add the chicken breasts to the pressure cooker and brown on both sides for 5 minutes each before removing from heat. Repeat for remaining chicken if there isn't enough room to brown all at once.

3. Add 1 tablespoon oil and the onion and cook for 3 minutes. Add the minced garlic and cook for another minute. Add the Marsala wine and let simmer for 2 minutes.

4. Return the chicken, along with the parsley and chicken stock, to the cooker. Seal shut, select the High Pressure function, and let cook for 8 minutes.

5. Use the natural release method and slowly remove the lid once the pressure has left the cooker. Season with salt and pepper to taste before serving.

GO VEGAN! Replace the chicken with seitan and the chicken stock with Vegetable Stock (store-bought or from page 26).

HONEY SESAME CHICKEN

MAKES 3 SERVINGS ✦ PREP TIME: 5 MINUTES ✦ COOKING TIME: 10 MINUTES

Great as a standalone dish, this meal also goes great over a bed of white rice!

1 tablespoon olive oil

2 chicken breasts, boneless, skinless and diced

Salt and pepper to taste

1 garlic clove, minced

¼ cup yellow onion, diced

¼ teaspoon red pepper flakes

2 tablespoons ketchup

½ cup soy sauce

1 tablespoon cornstarch

2 tablespoons water

1 teaspoon sesame oil

1 teaspoon white vinegar

½ cup honey

1 green onion, chopped

Sesame seeds, toasted

1. Stovetop Pressure Cooker: Place over medium heat. Add oil. Electrical Pressure Cooker: Select the Sauté function. Add oil.

2. Season the chicken breast with salt and pepper and place in the pressure cooker pot once hot and let cook for 2 to 3 minutes, or until the onions are soft.

3. Add the red pepper flakes, ketchup, and soy sauce to the pressure cooker pot and mix well. Seal shut, select the High Pressure function and let cook for another 2 to 3 minutes. Turn the pressure cooker off and do a quick pressure release.

4. In a separate bowl, combine the cornstarch and water and add to the cooker, along with the sesame oil, vinegar, and honey. Stir well, add to the pressure cooker, and let simmer for 3 minutes.

5. Once the sauce has thickened, stir in the green onion and toasted sesame seeds. Serve over white rice.

INDIAN CHICKEN WITH TOASTED CASHEWS

MAKES 4 SERVINGS · **PREP TIME: 6 HOURS** · **COOKING TIME: 13 MINUTES**

This is a delicious dish that brings a little bit of heat without overwhelming the taste buds. Anybody with a nut allergy can simply remove cashews from the recipe and enjoy the Indian chicken by itself.

1 container plain Greek yogurt

3 garlic cloves, minced

2 jalapeño peppers, chopped and seeded

2 tablespoons curry powder

2 tablespoons fresh ginger root, peeled and chopped

½ teaspoon cinnamon, ground

½ teaspoon cayenne

Salt and pepper to taste

1 tablespoon butter

4 chicken pieces

1 cup roasted cashew nuts

1 cup chicken stock

1 onion, diced

1 carrot, sliced

1. Add the yogurt, garlic, peppers, curry, ginger, cinnamon, cayenne, salt and pepper to a bowl and mix well. Place the chicken in a baking dish and coat each piece evenly with the yogurt mixture. Cover the dish and refrigerate for at least 6 hours.

2. Place ½ cup cashews and ¼ cup stock into a food processor and grind until smooth. Chop the remaining cashews.

3. Stovetop Pressure Cooker: Place over medium heat. Add butter.
Electrical Pressure Cooker: Select the Sauté function. Add butter.

4. Once hot, add the chicken to the cooker and brown for 3 minutes on each side. Remove the chicken and add the carrots and onion. Cook for 3 minutes.

5. Return the chicken to the cooker, along with the carrots, remaining yogurt mixture and nut purée. Seal the cooker, select the High Pressure function, and let cook for 7 minutes.

6. Use the natural release method and slowly remove the lid once the pressure has left the cooker. Remove the chicken, season with salt and pepper to taste, and sprinkle with remaining cashews before serving.

LEMON CHICKEN

MAKES 4 SERVINGS ✦ PREP TIME: 10 MINUTES ✦ COOKING TIME: 15 MINUTES

Another simple staple, this was one of my favorite dishes growing up. I always preferred it with white rice, though it works just as well with the Creamy Mashed Potatoes with Sour Cream found on page 187.

1 garlic clove, minced

1 teaspoon thyme

1 sprig sage, chopped

¼ bundle cilantro leaves, chopped

3 tablespoons olive oil

1½ lemons, juiced

½ teaspoon salt

¼ teaspoon pepper

½ whole chicken, skinless and boneless

1. In a bowl, mix together the garlic, thyme, sage, cilantro, 2 tablespoons olive oil, lemon juice, salt, and pepper. Mix thoroughly and briefly set aside.

2. Place the chicken in a storage container and cover it with the mixture. Seal the container and place in the refrigerator to marinate for at least 2 hours.

3. Place 1 tablespoon olive oil and the chicken into the pressure cooker and brown each chicken piece for 5 to 7 minutes. Once browned, pour the remaining marinade on top of the chicken, close the cover, and select the High Pressure function. Let cook for about 12 minutes.

4. Use the quick-release method and slowly remove the lid once the pressure has left the cooker. Remove the chicken and place onto a sheet of foil. Wrap the foil tightly around the chicken.

5. While keeping the cover off, turn the cooker to high heat until half of the cooking liquid has reduced and has a slightly thick consistency. Return the chicken to the pot, reduce the heat to low, and mix the remaining cooking liquid onto and over the chicken. Let simmer before serving.

TANDOORI CHICKEN

MAKES 2 SERVINGS ✦ PREP TIME: 8 HOURS AND 5 MINUTES ✦ COOKING TIME: 7 MINUTES

This is one of those dishes that requires some experimenting on your part to see what you like for a side dish. Veggies and rich flavors bring out the best in this dish, though that doesn't do much to narrow down the field. I enjoy it served with a little bit of Creamy Cauliflower Soup (page 61) on the side, which might be a good place for you to start.

¾ cup plain low-fat gluten-free yogurt

¼ cup gluten-free sour cream

½ lime, juiced

¼ teaspoon ginger, ground

½ teaspoon chili powder

½ teaspoon coriander

½ teaspoon salt

¼ teaspoon cayenne pepper

2 pounds chicken pieces, skinless

1. Add the yogurt, sour cream, and lime juice to a bowl and mix well. Whisk in the ginger, chili powder, coriander, salt, and cayenne pepper. Set aside.

2. Place the chicken in a cooking dish, coat with the yogurt mixture, cover, and refrigerate for at least 8 hours. Cover the remaining yogurt mixture and refrigerate as well.

3. Pour the remaining yogurt mixture and the chicken into the pressure cooker, seal and select the High Pressure function. Let cook for 7 minutes.

4. Use the natural release method and slowly remove the lid once the pressure has left the cooker. Remove the chicken, evenly pour the remaining yogurt mixture over each piece, and serve.

Tip! – For added flavor and a little bit more crisp, place the meat in a baking dish and let broil in an oven for 1 to 2 minutes on each side.

GO VEGAN! Replace the chicken pieces with equal servings seitan.

GO PALEO! Replace the low-fat yogurt with equal servings cultured coconut milk and the sour cream with equal servings coconut sour cream.

THAI RED BEEF CURRY

MAKES 2 SERVINGS ✦ PREP TIME: 15 MINUTES ✦ COOKING TIME: 45 MINUTES

This dish goes great with the Cilantro Lime Rice found on page 184.

½ tablespoon vegetable oil

½ onion, peeled and sliced

½ red bell pepper, sliced

2 cloves garlic, minced

½ tablespoon ginger, crushed

½ can coconut milk

½ (4-ounce) can red curry paste

1½ pounds chuck roast beef

1 teaspoon salt

¼ cup chicken stock

½ tablespoon Tamari soy sauce

½ lime, juiced

Dried basil, minced

1. Stovetop Pressure Cooker: Place over medium heat. Add oil. Electrical Pressure Cooker: Select the Sauté function. Add oil.

2. Once heated, place the onion, red pepper, garlic, and ginger and let cook for 3 minutes.

3. Add the coconut milk and red curry paste to the pot, stir well, and let cook for another 5 minutes.

4. Season the beef with salt before adding it to the pressure cooker, along with the chicken stock and soy sauce. Mix well, being sure to coat the beef in the contents of the cooker. Seal the lid, select the High Pressure function, and let cook for 12 minutes.

5. Let sit for several minutes before doing a quick release. Add the lime juice to the mixture, stir, and taste to ensure proper seasoning. Sprinkle the dried basil over the curry before serving.

GO PALEO! Replace the Tamari soy sauce with equal servings coconut aminos.

GO VEGAN! Replace the chuck roast beef with equal servings tofu and the chicken stock with equal servings amount Vegetable Stock (store-bought or from page 26).

BEEF SHORT RIBS WITH ROSEMARY

MAKES 4 SERVINGS ✦ PREP TIME: 15 MINUTES ✦ COOKING TIME: 48 MINUTES

There is no better combination in than these short ribs served over the Creamy Mashed Potatoes with Sour Cream from page 187.

2 tablespoons olive oil

2 pounds short ribs

1 cup diced onion

4 garlic cloves, minced

2 cups beef stock

2 tablespoons parsley, chopped

3 tablespoons rosemary, chopped

1. Stovetop Pressure Cooker: Place over medium heat. Add 1 tablespoon oil. Electric Pressure Cooker: Select the Sauté function. Add 1 tablespoon oil.

2. Once heated, add the ribs to the pressure cooker and brown each side for about 5 minutes before removing and setting aside.

3. Add 1 tablespoon oil and the onions to the cooker and cook over medium heat for 3 minutes. Add the garlic and cook for another minute.

4. Return the ribs to the cooker, along with the beef stock, parsley, and rosemary. Seal the cooker, select the High Pressure function, and let cook for 35 minutes.

5. Use the natural release method and slowly remove the lid once the valve drops. Remove the ribs and pour the remaining contents of the cooker over them before serving.

CORNED BEEF

MAKES 4 SERVINGS ✦ PREP TIME: 5 MINUTES ✦ COOKING TIME: 1½ HOURS

A simple dish, this recipe shouldn't pose a problem to even the greenest cooks out there. And I of course have to mention that this dish goes perfectly with the Southern Cabbage from page 195.

1 (3 pounds) flat-cut corned beef brisket, trimmed

½ teaspoon pepper

½ bottle beer, preferably a lager

1 cup chicken broth

1 garlic clove, minced

1 onion, quartered

1 bay leaf

1 teaspoon pickling spices

1. Season the corned beef with pepper and place in the pressure cooker. Add the remaining ingredients, seal the cooker, select the High Pressure function, and let cook for 1½ hours.

2. Use the natural release method and slowly remove the lid once the pressure has left the cooker. Remove the corned beef and let sit for several minutes before slicing and serving.

GO GLUTEN FREE! Make sure that the beer you're using is gluten-free!

POT ROAST

MAKES 6 SERVINGS ✦ PREP TIME: 20 MINUTES ✦ COOKING TIME: 1 HOUR AND 20 MINUTES

I find that this recipe includes the combination of flavors that best complement the beef chuck roast. This dish can be served with most anything, though it works best for me when served with green vegetables.

2 tablespoons vegetable oil

1 (3 pound) beef chuck roast, boneless

½ teaspoon salt

½ teaspoon pepper

1 onion, halved and sliced

3 garlic cloves, minced

3 basil sprigs

2 cups beef broth

1½ tablespoons Worcestershire sauce

4 potatoes, peeled and cubed

4 carrots, peeled and sliced

1. Stovetop Pressure Cooker: Place over medium heat. Add oil.
   Electrical Pressure Cooker: Select the Sauté function. Add oil.

2. Season the beef with salt and pepper and, when hot, place in the pressure cooker. Brown for 3 minutes on each side. Remove from the cooker and set aside.

3. Add the onion to the cooker and cook for 3 minutes. Return the beef, along with the garlic, basil, broth, and Worcestershire sauce to the cooker. Seal shut, select the High Pressure function, and let cook for 1 hour.

4. Use the quick-release method and slowly remove the lid once the pressure has left the cooker. Add the potatoes and carrots, seal the cooker, and cook on high heat for 12 minutes.

5. Use the natural release method and slowly remove the lid once the pressure has left the cooker. Remove the beef and pour the remaining cooker contents over the top before serving.

I doubt that many people will have tried this meal more than a few times in their life, and to them I say to work this recipe into your schedule more often. The final product is sweet, savory and delicious.

HAWAIIAN-STYLE PORK

MAKES 4 SERVINGS ✦ PREP TIME: 5 MINUTES ✦ COOKING TIME: 1½ HOURS

One of the more unique recipes in the book, this combination of salty and savory tastes is a perfect go-to for any occasion.

2½ pounds pork roast

3 garlic cloves, minced

½ yellow onion, diced

½ tablespoon red Hawaiian fine salt

½ teaspoon black pepper

1 cup water

Grilled pineapple rings

1. Cut the pork roast into fourths and place in the pressure cooker. Add in the garlic, onion, salt, pepper, and water. Seal cooker, select the High Pressure function, and then let cook for 1½ hours.

2. Use the natural release method and slowly remove the lid once the pressure has left the cooker. Remove the pork and shred with two forks. Serve with grilled pineapple rings.

Tips! – For some added flavor, sear the pork with a thin coating of oil in a pan over medium-high heat for several minutes on each side. – Make it a kebab! For utensil free eating simply cut the pork and pineapple rings into equal sized pieces, line up as desired, and spear with a kebab!

GO VEGAN! Substitute the pork for equal servings tempeh.

HERBED PORK ROAST

MAKES 4 SERVINGS ✦ PREP TIME: 15 MINUTES ✦ COOKING TIME: 31 MINUTES

This dish goes well with any number of sides, so mix it up a little bit. Try serving it with the Summer Squash With Cilantro and Basil from page 180.

3 cloves garlic, minced

½ teaspoon salt

½ teaspoon pepper

2 tablespoons rosemary, chopped

1 tablespoon fresh parsley

1 tablespoon sage, chopped

1½ pounds pork roast, boneless

1 tablespoon vegetable oil

2 celery ribs, chopped

1 cup chicken stock

1. Mix together the garlic, salt, pepper, rosemary, parsley, and sage in a bowl. Coat the pork roast with the mixture.

2. Stovetop Pressure Cooker: Place over medium heat. Add oil.
   Electrical Pressure Cooker: Select the Sauté function. Add oil.

3. Once heated, add the pork to the cooker and brown for 3 minutes on each side. Add the celery and the chicken stock to the cooker, seal, select the High Pressure function, and cook for 25 minutes.

4. Use the natural release method and slowly remove the lid once the pressure has left the cooker. Season with salt and pepper to taste before serving.

GO VEGAN!   Replace the pork roast with tempeh and the chicken stock with Vegetable Stock (store-bought or from page 26).

PORK CARNITAS TACOS WITH AVOCADO AND SOUR CREAM

MAKES 5 SERVINGS ✦ PREP TIME: 10 MINUTES ✦ COOKING TIME: 55 MINUTES

This dish can be served with rice and peas if desired, though I think that it works better as a standalone meal. Avocado and sour cream are my preferred toppings, but you can certainly tailor this to your liking.

1 pound pork, boneless

1 teaspoon salt

1 teaspoon black pepper

½ teaspoon garlic powder

½ teaspoon cumin

¼ teaspoon Goya Sazon

¼ teaspoon thyme

¼ cup chicken broth

¼ can Goya Chipotle Peppers in Adobo Sauce

¼ teaspoon Goya Adobo Seasoning

5 mini taco shells

1 avocado, sliced

Sour cream

1. Season the pork in salt and pepper, brown in a skillet over high heat for 4 minutes, and set aside to cool.

2. Once the pork has cooled, season with garlic powder, cumin, Sazon, and ⅛ teaspoon thyme.

3. In the pressure cooker, mix together the remaining thyme, chicken broth, and chipotle peppers in adobo sauce. Add the pork, seal the lid, select the High Pressure function, and let cook for 45 minutes.

4. Turn off the pressure cooker and let sit for 5 minutes. Use the quick-release method to release the pressure and remove the pork from the cooker. Shred the pork with a fork and then mix it with the juices at the bottom of the cooker, adding the adobo seasoning while mixing.

5. Remove the juicy pork from the cooker and add to flour tortilla. Add your desired quantities of avocado slices and sour cream to the tacos and enjoy.

GO VEGETARIAN! Replace the pork with tempeh.

GO VEGAN! Replace the pork with tempeh and serve without sour cream.

SPICY SAUSAGE AND PEPPERS

MAKES 3 SERVINGS ✦ PREP TIME: 5 MINUTES ✦ COOKING TIME: 30 MINUTES

A classic dish, consider serving this with the Herbed Tomato Sauce found on page 41.

5 sweet Italian sausages

2 red peppers, seeded and cut into strips

2 green peppers, seeded and cut into strips

2 tomatoes, diced

½ can tomato sauce

½ cup water

½ tablespoon oregano

2 teaspoons garlic, minced

1. Place the sausages and peppers into the pressure cooker and set aside.

2. In a bowl, mix together the tomatoes, tomato sauce, water, oregano, and garlic. Pour the mixture into the pressure cooker over the sausage and peppers. Close the cover, select the High Pressure function, and let cook for 30 minutes.

3. After 30 minutes, turn off the pressure cooker and use a quick-release. Remove the cover once the pressure has been released and remove the contents to serve.

GO VEGAN!   Replace sausages with Boca Italian Meatless Sausages.

GO GLUTEN-FREE!   Make sure the sausages that you're using are gluten-free before purchasing them. Look at the sausage casings especially!

SWEET BARBECUE PORK

MAKES 4 SERVINGS ✦ PREP TIME: 5 MINUTES ✦ COOKING TIME: 15 MINUTES

I'm a sucker for pairing anything that includes barbecue flavoring with the Red Potatoes side from page 192. I find that they're only complete with generous amounts of salt and butter, which complement the barbecue sauce especially well!

2 pounds pork ribs

2 garlic cloves, minced

Salt and pepper to taste

1 cup chicken stock

1 cup Sweet Baby Ray's Barbecue Sauce

1. Season the pork with the garlic, salt, and pepper before adding to the pressure cooker. Add the chicken stock, seal shut, select the High Pressure function, and let cook for 15 minutes.

2. Use the natural release method and slowly remove the lid once the pressure has left the cooker. While the pressure is dropping, pour the barbecue sauce into a large bowl. Remove the pork, place in the bowl, and cover with barbecue sauce before serving.

Tip! – For an extra char on your ribs, remove them from the pressure cooker 5 minutes before they are finished and transfer them to a stovetop grill. Grill on each side for 3 minutes, and serve immediately.

GO VEGETARIAN! Replace the pork with equal servings tempeh and the chicken stock with Vegetable Stock (store-bought or from page 26).

GO VEGAN! Replace the pork with tempeh and the chicken stock with Vegetable Stock (store-bought or from page 26).

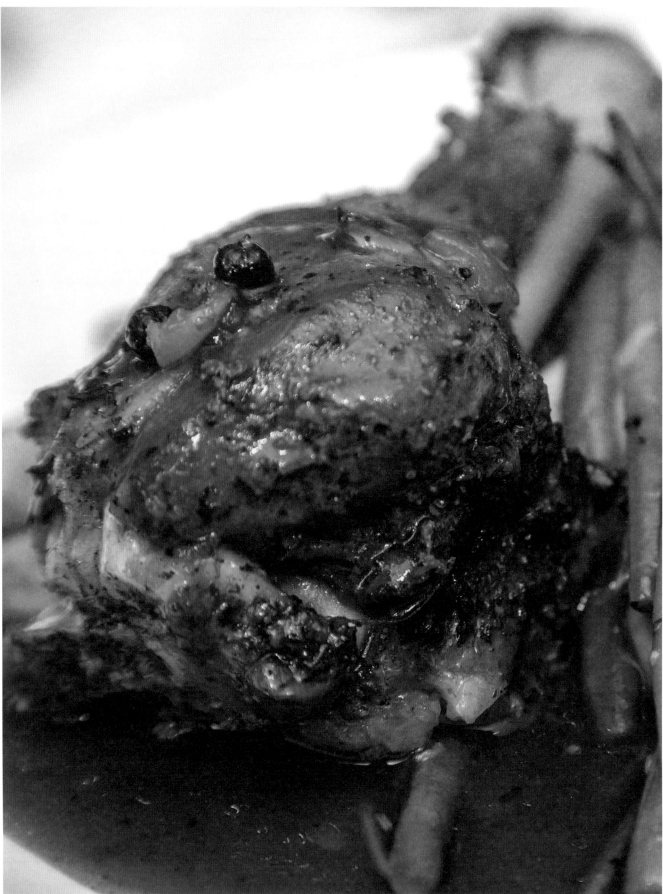

LAMB SHANKS

MAKES 2 SERVINGS ✦ PREP TIME: 10 MINUTES ✦ COOKING TIME: 50 MINUTES

Don't let the simplicity of this dish fool you; there are plenty of flavors here that make this recipe a must try.

1½ pounds lamb shanks

Salt and pepper to taste

2 tablespoons olive oil

1 celery stalk, chopped

½ large yellow onion, chopped

½ tablespoon tomato paste

1½ cloves garlic, minced

1½ tomatoes, diced

½ cup bone broth

½ tablespoon balsamic vinegar

1. Season the lamb shanks with salt and pepper and, along with 1 tablespoon olive oil, add to the pressure cooker. Select the High Pressure function and cook for 8 minutes on all sides, until brown.

2. Use the quick-release method and, when the pressure has left the cooker, remove the lamb. Add the remaining olive oil, celery, and onion, seal, and select the Low Pressure function. Cook for 3 minutes before mixing in the tomato paste, garlic, tomatoes, bone broth, and vinegar to the cooker. Return the lamb shanks to cooker, seal the lid, and return to high pressure. Once high pressure is achieved, lower the heat while maintaining the pressure and let cook for 40 minutes.

3. After 40 minutes, turn off the cooker and let the pressure drop naturally. Remove the lamb shanks and place them on a serving platter, pouring the sauce from the cooker over them before serving.

MINI TURKEY MEATBALLS WITH EGGPLANT

MAKES MAKES ABOUT 25 MEATBALLS ◆ PREP TIME: 30 MINUTES ◆ COOKING TIME: 5 MINUTES

Serve these with the Herbed Tomato Sauce from page 41.

½ pound ground turkey

1 egg, lightly beaten

1 tablespoon olive oil

1 tablespoon Romano cheese, grated

1 onion, chopped

1 teaspoon dried oregano

1 teaspoon dried basil

1½ garlic cloves, minced

½ teaspoon salt

½ pepper

2 large eggplants, thinly sliced

2 large tomatoes, quartered and crushed

1. In a large bowl, mix together the turkey, egg, olive oil, cheese, onion, oregano, basil, garlic, salt, and pepper. Stir until the mixture is consistent throughout. Form meatballs from the mixture that are all close in size.

2. Place the sliced eggplant into the pressure cooker. Place the meatballs on top, followed by the crushed tomatoes. Seal, select the High Pressure function, and let cook for 5 minutes.

3. Use the natural release method and slowly remove the lid once the pressure has left the cooker. Season with salt and pepper to taste before serving.

GO VEGETARIAN! Replace the turkey with equal servings seitan.

GO GLUTEN-FREE AND PALEO! Skip the cheese in the meatball mixture.

MUSSELS WITH LEMON AND GARLIC

MAKES 2 SERVINGS   **PREP TIME: 10 MINUTES**   **COOKING TIME: 3 MINUTES**

As with all seafood dishes, lemon and garlic are the perfect complementary flavors here to the mussels!

1 tablespoon olive oil

½ onion, diced

1 garlic clove, minced

1 pound fresh mussels, cleaned and de-bearded

¼ cup dry white wine

½ cup chicken broth

½ lemon, juiced

Fresh dill, chopped

1. Stovetop Pressure Cooker: Place over medium heat. Add oil. Electrical Pressure Cooker: Select the Sauté function. Add oil.

2. Once heated, add the onion and garlic. Let cook for 2 minutes, stirring occasionally.

3. Add the mussels, wine, broth, and lemon juice, seal shut, select the Low Pressure function, and let cook for 3 minutes

4. Use the quick-release method and slowly remove the lid once the pressure has left the cooker. Season with fresh dill before serving.

Tip! – Feel free to replace the wine with seafood stock.

SALMON WITH SPICY SALSA TOPPING

MAKES 4 SERVINGS ✦ PREP TIME: 5 MINUTES ✦ COOKING TIME: 2 MINUTES

Serving this dish with a side of white rice does well to complement the spicy salsa topping that made me fall in love with this dish in the first place.

2 cloves garlic, minced

2 tablespoons coriander, ground

2 tablespoons chili powder

½ teaspoon salt

½ teaspoon pepper

4 salmon steaks, fresh

2 tablespoons olive oil

¼ jalapeño chili, stemmed, seeded and minced

3 plum tomatoes, cored, chopped and seeded

¼ cup red onion, chopped

2 limes, juiced

1. In a small bowl, combine the garlic, coriander, chili powder, salt, and pepper. Set aside.

2. Brush each salmon steak with olive oil and coat in the garlic mixture before adding to the pressure cooker. Seal the cooker, select the High Pressure function, and let cook for 2 minutes.

3. Use the quick-release method and slowly remove the lid once the pressure has left the cooker. Remove salmon and briefly set aside.

4. In a separate bowl, combine the jalapeños, tomatoes, onions, and lime juice and mix well. Serve on top of or to the side of the salmon steaks.

Tip! – For complementary flavor, serve over a bed of white rice!

GO VEGAN! Replace the salmon steaks with equal servings Gardein Golden Fishless Filets.

SWORDFISH WITH LEMON AND CAPERS

MAKES 4-6 SERVINGS ✦ PREP TIME: 5 MINUTES ✦ COOKING TIME: 4 MINUTES

Like the salmon, I find that this dish works best with a side of white rice.

3 tablespoons
unsalted butter

2 lemons, ends removed,
sliced and seeded

2 tablespoons capers

3 pounds
swordfish steak

1 tablespoon
dill, chopped

Salt and pepper to taste

1. Stovetop Pressure Cooker: Place over medium heat. Add butter. Electrical Pressure Cooker: Select the Sauté function. Add butter.

2. Once heated, add the lemons and the capers and cook until the capers are heated through, about 1 minute.

3. Add the swordfish steak to the cooker, seal, select the High Pressure function and, if using a stovetop cooker, cook on as low a heat as possible while maintaining the high pressure. Let cook for 3 minutes.

4. Use the natural release method and slowly remove the lid once the pressure has left the cooker. Season the swordfish with dill, salt, and pepper to taste before serving.

GO VEGAN! Replace the swordfish steak with equal servings Gardein's golden fishless filets.

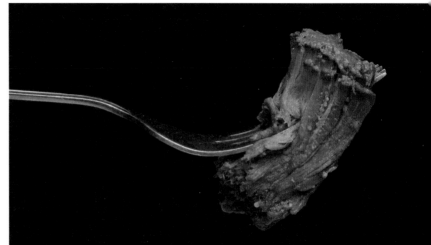

SIDES

I've always had an affinity for the side dish. I was a very picky eater growing up and had to rely on the mashed potatoes, French fries and refried beans for sustenance whenever we went out to eat. While my pallet has obviously expanded over the last several years, I'm still a sucker for a good side dish. To this day I still find myself getting more excited for the garlic mashed potatoes than I do for the steak that accompanies them. So, needless to say, I've put a lot of time into coming up with some of my favorite side dish recipes to share with you. They're all easy to make, diet-friendly, and fun to play with! Try these sides with different recipes from the Main Dishes section to find your favorite combinations.

You'll also find that a lot of these dishes are very diet-friendly. The majority don't contain meat, few contain dairy, and about half can be part of a Paleo diet. Legumes and veggies were the main focus here; they're easy to make and very consumer-friendly. That said, having a good mix was important as well, which is why you'll find a few recipes featuring bacon in this section.

Here we have a cultivation of substantive sides that do well to complement certain entrées that they can be served with. They're not overpowering; you'll find that few ingredients are needed to make most of these dishes. In fact, this might be the place to start if you're new to pressure cooking. Above all, this is the section where little investment equals high reward!

BLACK BEANS

MAKES 6 SERVINGS ✦ PREP TIME: 5 MINUTES ✦ COOKING TIME: 35 MINUTES

A simple side with a simple recipe, this is a great place to start for somebody who doesn't have much experience with a pressure cooker.

6 tablespoons olive oil

1½ onions, diced

3 cloves garlic, minced

1 bay leaf

3 cups black beans, soaked overnight

9 cups water

1. Stovetop Pressure Cookers: Place over medium heat. Add 3 tablespoons oil. Electrical Pressure Cooker: Select the Sauté function. Add 3 tablespoons oil.

2. Once heated, add the onions to the pressure cooker and let cook for 3 minutes, or until the onions are translucent.

3. Add the garlic and the bay leaf to the cooker and cook for another 90 seconds. Mix in the black beans, water, 3 tablespoons oil, and a pinch of salt and pepper. Seal the cooker, select the High Pressure function and, if using a stovetop cooker, cook on as low a heat as possible while maintaining the pressure. Let cook for 30 minutes.

4. Use the quick-release method and slowly remove the lid once the pressure has left the cooker. Remove the bay leaf and discard. Season to taste before serving.

Tip! – Reduce your cooking time to 6 minutes by soaking your beans for 8 to 12 hours before preparing this dish.

REFRIED BEANS

MAKES 6 SERVINGS ✦ PREP TIME: 5 MINUTES ✦ COOKING TIME: 43 MINUTES

My favorite side for Spanish cuisine, these refried beans are absolutely delicious. Make note of how their consistency turns out after making them once so that you know what to adjust for next time. These beans go great with a sprinkle of grated cheddar cheese on top!

6 cups dried pinto beans, soaked and rinsed

5 cups water

1 tablespoon vegetable oil

2 onions, chopped

6 garlic cloves, chopped

3 teaspoons basil

2 teaspoons dried cumin

1 teaspoon pepper

¼ cup vegetable shortening

5 cups Vegetable Stock (store-bought or page 26)

1½ teaspoons salt

1. Stovetop Pressure Cooker: Place over medium heat. Add oil. Electrical Pressure Cooker: Select the Sauté function. Add oil.

2. Once hot, add the chopped onion. Let cook for 3 minutes. Add the garlic, basil, cumin, pepper, vegetable shortening, vegetable stock, water, and beans. Stir well. Seal shut, select the Bean/Chili function, and let cook for 40 minutes.

3. Use the natural release method and slowly remove the lid once the pressure has left the cooker. Stir the beans and salt to taste. If necessary, add the beans to a food processor and blend until the desired consistency is achieved. Let cool for several minutes before serving.

Tip! – Reduce your cooking time to 6 minutes by soaking your beans for 8 to 12 hours before preparing this dish.

CHEESE GRITS

MAKES 2 SERVINGS ✦ PREP TIME: 5 MINUTES ✦ COOKING TIME: 15 MINUTES

Delicious with any dish, this serving of Southern comfort can serve as a meal if necessary. Otherwise, try to pair with dishes that won't be overwhelmed by the cheese and butter featured here!

2 cups water

2 tablespoons butter

½ cup Stone Ground Grits or cornmeal

¾ teaspoon salt

½ teaspoon pepper

½ cup sharp cheddar cheese, shredded

1. Add the water, butter, grits, salt, and pepper to the pressure cooker, stir well, and secure lid. Select the Low Pressure function and let cook for 15 minutes.

2. Use the natural release method and slowly remove the lid once the pressure has left the cooker. Add the cheese and mix well. Let sit for a minute before serving.

FRIED RICE WITH CARROTS

MAKES 2 SERVINGS ✦ PREP TIME: 10 MINUTES ✦ COOKING TIME: 15 MINUTES

A classic side dish for those of us familiar with takeout, this homemade alternative should be served with a side of low-sodium soy sauce.

1½ cups water

½ carrot, chopped and diced

1 cup long grain rice

¼ cup corn, not frozen

¼ teaspoon salt

1 tablespoon canola oil

5 scallions, chopped

1 egg, beaten

1. Add the water, carrots, rice, corn, and salt to the pressure cooker, seal shut, select the High Pressure function, and cook for 12 minutes.

2. Use the natural release method and slowly remove the lid once the pressure has left the cooker. Stir well.

3. Select the Sauté function if using an electric cooker, or place over high heat if using a stovetop cooker. Add the oil, scallions and egg to the mixture and stir well. Stir occasionally until cooked.

COLLARD GREENS WITH BACON

MAKES 4 SERVINGS ✦ PREP TIME: 7 MINUTES ✦ COOKING TIME: 30 MINUTES

Be wary of sodium content here, as it can get out of hand pretty quickly once you add more seasoning!

1 tablespoon vegetable oil

¼ pound bacon strips, sliced into 1-inch pieces

¾ pound collard greens, rinsed with stems trimmed

½ teaspoon salt

½ cup water

Pepper to taste

1. Stovetop Pressure Cooker: Place over medium heat. Add oil. Electrical Pressure Cooker: Select the Sauté function. Add oil.

2. Once hot, add the bacon and cook until crispy, about 5 minutes. Slowly start to stir in the collard greens one handful at a time, adding another once the greens in the cooker begin to wilt. Once all of the greens are in, add water and season with salt. Seal shut, select the High Pressure function, and let cook for 20 minutes.

3. Use the quick-release method and slowly remove the lid once the valve has dropped. Let sit for one minute. Season with pepper to taste before serving.

SUMMER SQUASH WITH CILANTRO AND BASIL

MAKES 2 SERVINGS ♦ PREP TIME: 1 MINUTE ♦ COOKING TIME: 1½ MINUTES

A very delicious and healthy side, squash is the perfect ingredient to mix and match with different herbs and flavors.

1 tablespoon vegetable oil

1 clove garlic, minced

1 tablespoon cilantro, chopped

1 tablespoon basil, chopped

2 tablespoons red pepper, diced

1 tablespoon Vegetable Stock (store-bought or from page 26)

1½ cups summer squash, sliced

Salt and pepper to taste

1. Stovetop Pressure Cooker: Place over medium heat. Add oil. Electrical Pressure Cooker: Select the Sauté function. Add oil.

2. Once hot, add the garlic and let cook for 30 seconds, stirring constantly. Add the cilantro, basil, and red pepper and cook for another 30 seconds, still stirring constantly. Add the vegetable stock and the squash, seal the cover, place on the lowest pressure possible, and let cook for 45 seconds.

3. Use the quick release function and slowly remove the lid once all of the pressure has left the cooker. Pour the contents in a separate dish and season with salt and pepper to taste before serving.

SWEET POTATO HASH WITH BLACK BEANS AND AVOCADO SLICES

MAKES 2 SERVINGS ✦ PREP TIME: 3 MINUTES ✦ COOKING TIME: 8 MINUTES

What could just as easily be a breakfast item has become one of my favorite and go-to pressure cooker recipes. The avocados really put it over the top for me, though you should garnish as you see fit.

1 tablespoon vegetable oil

½ green onion, chopped

1 clove garlic, minced

1 cup sweet potato, peeled and chopped

¼ cup Vegetable Stock (store-bought or from page 26)

½ cup black beans, cooked

Salt and pepper to taste

¼ avocado, sliced

1. Stovetop Pressure Cooker: Place over medium heat. Add oil.
   Electrical Pressure Cooker: Select the Sauté function. Add oil.

2. Once hot, add the onion and cook for 3 minutes. Add the garlic and cook for another minute, stirring occasionally. Mix in the sweet potatoes and the stock. Seal shut, select the High Pressure function, and let cook for 2½ minutes.

3. Use the quick-release method and slowly remove the lid once all of the pressure leaves the cooker. Add the black beans and repeat the cooking process in step 2.

4. Repeat the release process in step 3, remove the contents of the cooker and top with avocado slices before serving.

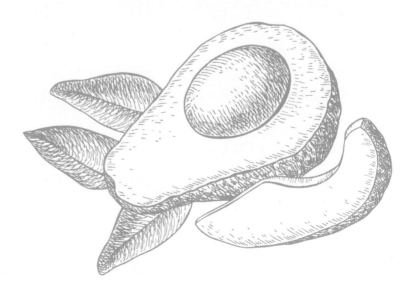

CILANTRO LIME RICE

MAKES 4 SERVINGS   **PREP TIME: 5 MINUTES**   **COOKING TIME: 8 MINUTES**

I've found that this side goes particularly well with the seafood entrees, as well as any recipe featuring Spanish cuisine.

2 cups long grain white rice

2½ cups water

¼ cup vegetable oil

1½ teaspoons salt

2 tablespoons fresh lime juice

⅓ cup fresh cilantro, chopped

1. Add the rice, water, and oil into the pressure cooker, seal shut, select the High Pressure function and let cook for 8 minutes.

2. Use a quick-release method and slowly remove the lid once the valve has dropped. Fluff the rice.

3. In a separate bowl, combine the salt, lime juice, and cilantro and mix well. Add the rice, stir to combine and serve warm.

CREAMY MASHED POTATOES WITH SOUR CREAM

MAKES 4-6 SERVINGS ✦ PREP TIME: 2 MINUTES ✦ COOKING TIME: 10 MINUTES

Who doesn't love a good side of mashed potatoes? A staple for a lot of people growing up, this dish can serve as a very good bed for a lot of recipes in this book.

4 pounds Russet potatoes, peeled and diced

1½ cup water

1½ cup milk

1 stick butter

¾ cup gluten-free sour cream

Salt and pepper to taste

1. Place the potatoes and water into the pressure cooker, seal, select the High Pressure function and let cook for 7 minutes. Use the quick-release method and slowly remove the lid once the pressure has left the cooker.

2. Place the milk and butter in a small pot and place over medium heat, until the butter is completely melted.

3. Empty the contents of the cooker into a bowl and mix in the butter and milk mixture. Stir until the mixture is smooth and the lumps are gone. Add sour cream, salt, and pepper and mix well.

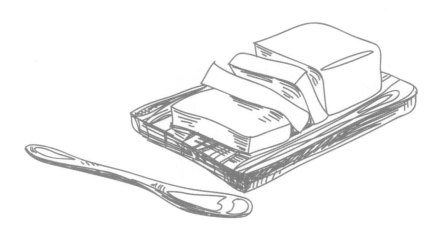

CURRY RICE PILAF WITH PEAS AND CARROTS

MAKES 2 SERVINGS ✦ PREP TIME: 2 MINUTES ✦ COOKING TIME: 5 MINUTES

Here is a delicious side that features a bit of a kick depending on how much curry powder is added! Keep spice in mind when finding a dish to pair this with.

½ tablespoon salted butter

1 cup water

½ teaspoon salt

⅛ teaspoon curry powder

2 tablespoons frozen peas

2 tablespoons carrots, diced

½ cup Basmati rice

1. Place all the ingredients into the pressure cooker, seal, and select the High Pressure function. Let cook for 5 minutes.

2. Let sit for several minutes before using the quick-release method. Slowly remove the lid once the pressure has left the cooker and the pilaf should be ready to serve.

LOADED MAC AND CHEESE

MAKES 2-3 SERVINGS ✦ PREP TIME: 10 MINUTES ✦ COOKING TIME: 40 MINUTES

I know, I know. This is quite the side. Feel free to serve it by itself, but when I'm feeling really hungry, I find that it goes well with pretty much anything featuring barbecue sauce.

1 cup elbow macaroni

2 cups water

¼ teaspoon salt

1 large egg, beaten

1½ cups milk

½ teaspoon dry mustard

½ teaspoon hot sauce

2 tablespoons salted butter

1 cup sharp cheddar, grated

½ cup American cheese, grated

4 strips bacon, cooked crispy and crumbled

¼ cup breadcrumbs, cooked golden brown

1. Add the macaroni, water, and salt to the pressure cooker, cover, and select the High Pressure function. Let cook for 4 minutes. Use the natural release method and slowly remove the lid once the pressure has left the cooker. Let sit for several minutes.

2. In a separate bowl, mix together the egg, milk, dry mustard, and hot sauce. Set aside.

3. Select the Keep Warm function on the electric pressure cooker (leave over low heat for the stovetop pressure cooker) and add the salted butter to the macaroni. Stir in the mixture from step 2 and mix well. Add half of the quantities of both cheeses to the macaroni, stir until melted, and repeat with the remaining cheese.

4. Sprinkle the crumbled bacon, breadcrumbs, salt and pepper over the macaroni before serving.

GO VEGETARIAN!   Serve without the bacon crisps.

RED POTATOES

MAKES 4 SERVINGS ✦ PREP TIME: 2 MINUTES ✦ COOKING TIME: 10 MINUTES

Red potatoes, while very simple, have always been a favorite of mine. They are versatile enough to go well with almost any sauce or marinade involved with your entrée.

2 tablespoons
vegetable oil

1 dozen medium
red potatoes, washed

2 cups chicken stock

Salt and pepper to taste

1. Add the olive oil to the pressure cooker, followed by the red potatoes and chicken stock. Seal the cooker, select High Pressure, and let cook for 10 minutes.

2. Use the natural release method and slowly remove the lid once the pressure has left the cooker. Season with salt and pepper before serving.

Tip! – For an extra char to your potatoes, transfer from the pressure cooker to a stovetop grill immediately after cooking. Grill over high-heat for about 4 minutes, or until your potatoes develop soft grill marks. Serve immediately!

GO VEGAN! Replace the chicken stock with equal amount Vegetable Stock (store-bought or from page 26).

SOUTHERN CABBAGE

MAKES 3 SERVINGS ✦ PREP TIME: 20 MINUTES ✦ COOKING TIME: 10 MINUTES

I find, not surprisingly, that this side goes well with the Corned Beef recipe from page 142.

1 head cabbage, cored and cut into 1-inch pieces

¼ cup salted butter

2 cups Vegetable Stock (store-bought or from page 26)

Salt and pepper to taste

1. Place the cabbage, butter, and vegetable stock into the cooker and mix well. Seal the cooker, select the High Pressure function and cook for 3 minutes.

2. Use the natural release method and slowly remove the lid once the pressure has left the cooker. Season with salt and pepper to taste before serving.

GO VEGAN!   Replace the butter with equal servings of olive oil.

STEWED GREEN BEANS WITH GARLIC

MAKES 2 SERVINGS ✦ PREP TIME: 5 MINUTES ✦ COOKING TIME: 8 MINUTES

A very simple recipe that yields a very delicious side, this dish can accompany almost any entrée and complement it well.

1½ tablespoons vegetable oil

½ garlic clove, minced

1 cup water

½ pound green beans, fresh

½ teaspoon salt

1 teaspoon basil, crushed

1. Add 1 tablespoon vegetable oil and the garlic to the pressure cooker and cook on medium heat for 3 minutes.

2. Add water to the pressure cooker. Add the green beans to the steamer basket, sprinkle salt, and add to the pressure cooker. Seal the cooker, select the High Pressure function and, if using a stovetop cooker, cook on the lowest possible heat while maintaining the high pressure. Let cook for 5 minutes.

3. Use the quick-release method and slowly remove the lid once the pressure has left the cooker. Pour the green beans into the base of the cooker and mix with the garlic. Mix well and remove the green beans from the cooker.

4. Sprinkle the basil and remaining vegetable oil over the beans and serve.

DESSERTS

As we all know, no meal is complete if it doesn't end with dessert. Featured ahead are the best dishes with which to end a day, from the healthy to the…. not so much. And, while the range of pressure cooker desserts is slightly limited, there are still plenty of sweet options out there are well worth trying. I've done my best to cultivate some of those options for you ahead!

You'll find that this section is a little bit fruit heavy, which was my intent. Dishes like Baked Apples and Cinnamon Stewed Fruits offer us a delicious final course without being too heavy. Not to mention the fact that the pressure cooker is an excellent tool when it comes to preparing fruits for dishes like these.

Of course, you'll also find some recipes in there that appear to be a bit more challenging than the rest of the section. Don't worry about it! They're not as intimidating as they seem, and a messed up kitchen session here doesn't end up costing you very much time or money at all. It's fun to make (and eat) Pressure-Cooker Chocolate Cake. And I believe that everybody should try cooking Crème Brulee once in their life, a goal that I've made a whole lot easier for you thanks to the recipe found a few pages away.

BAKED APPLES

MAKES 3 SERVINGS ✦ PREP TIME: 7 MINUTES ✦ COOKING TIME: 20 MINUTES

These were the first baked apples I'd ever had and I haven't looked back since. It's a delicious desert and is actually pretty healthy.

3 fresh red apples, cored

2 tablespoons raisins

2 tablespoons walnut pieces

½ cup red wine

¼ cup brown sugar

½ teaspoon cinnamon powder

1. Place the apples into the pressure cooker and pour in the raisins, walnuts, wine, brown sugar, and cinnamon powder. Seal the lid and cook for 10 minutes on High Pressure.

2. Use the natural release method and slowly remove the lid once the pressure has left the cooker. Remove and serve.

Tip! – For our friends who are gluten-free, make sure that the cinnamon powder is gluten-free before purchasing.

GO PALEO! Replace the brown sugar with ⅛ cup maple syrup.

CREAMY RICE PUDDING

Here we have a rather unique cooking process relative to the rest of the book, so be sure to read closely on this one!

¾ cups Arborio
or Sushi rice

¼ teaspoon salt

2½ cups whole milk

½ cup sugar

1 egg

¾ teaspoon
vanilla extract

½ cup half and half

1. Stovetop Pressure Cooker: Place over medium heat.
   Electrical Pressure Cooker: Select the Sauté function.

2. Combine rice, salt, milk, and sugar in pressure cooker pot and stir the mixture constantly until it is brought to a boil, at which point stop stirring and close the lid. Select the Low Pressure function and let cook for 15 minutes.

3. In a bowl, whisk the egg together with the vanilla extract and half and half. Set aside.

4. Use the natural release method and slowly remove the lid once the pressure has left the cooker. Stir the egg mixture into the contents of the pot.

5. Once the contents of the pot are thoroughly mixed, bring to a boil uncovered. Once boiling, turn the pressure cooker off and stir again.

6. Serve immediately or pour the contents into a container and chill for several hours.

Add some flavor! Stir ½ cup of raisins in after final boil or sprinkle with cinnamon on top before serving.

TEACUP CRÈME BRULEE

MAKES 3 SERVINGS ✦ PREP TIME: 3 ½ HOURS ✦ COOKING TIME: 6 MINUTES

Making crème brulee can seem like a daunting task, but it really isn't. Follow the steps below to produce my favorite dessert in the book.

4 egg yolks

¼ cup granulated sugar

½ teaspoon salt

½ cup whole milk

½ cup heavy cream

1 teaspoon vanilla

1 cup water

1 tablespoon vegetable oil

3 tablespoons raw sugar

1. In a large bowl, whisk together egg yolks, granulated sugar, salt, milk, cream, and vanilla. Whisk until thoroughly mixed. Set aside.

2. Add the water to the pressure cooking pot and secure the trivet in the bottom of the cooker.

3. Oil the sides of three teacups and carefully pour the mixture into each. Give each a little stir, being careful not to spill. Cover each cup with foil, place in the cooker, secure the lid, select the High Pressure function and let cook for 6 minutes.

4. Use the natural release method and slowly remove the lid once the pressure has left the cooker. Remove the teacups and set aside to cool for another 30 minutes. Once cool, refrigerate for at least 3 hours or up to a day and a half.

5. When ready to serve, sprinkle the top of each dessert with sugar, being careful to distribute evenly. Move the flame of the culinary torch in a circular motion several inches above the surface of each dessert until the tops are caramelized. Serve and enjoy!

Tip! – Don't have a culinary torch? An oven broiler should serve as a suitable substitute! Keep them under the broiler for about 7 minutes, rotating frequently so as to evenly distribute the heat.

VANILLA SPICED POACHED PLUMS

MAKES 2 CUPS ✦ PREP TIME: 5 MINUTES ✦ COOKING TIME: 26 MINUTES

Here we have a rather unique cooking process relative to the rest of the book, so be sure to read closely on this one!

1 cup water

2 tablespoons honey

2 cinnamon sticks, ground

2 cardamom pods

1 star anise

1 vanilla bean pod, split and seeded

3 cloves

10 small fresh plums, split and pitted

1. Place all ingredients into the pressure cooker, seal shut, select the High Pressure function, and let cook for 20 minutes.

2. Use the natural release method and slowly remove the lid once the pressure has left the cooker. Remove the plums and set aside.

3. Select the Sauté function or, if you're using a stovetop cooker, place over low heat and let the remaining contents simmer for 6 minutes. Pour over the plums and serve, or refrigerate and serve cold.

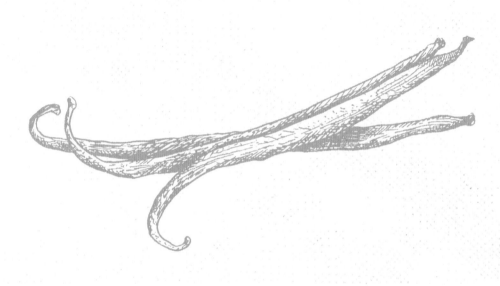

CINNAMON STEWED FRUITS

MAKES 3 SERVINGS ✦ PREP TIME: 10 MINUTES ✦ COOKING TIME: 20 MINUTES

A delicious dessert, the fruits should be served with whipped cream if diet isn't an issue.

½ cinnamon stick, sliced

1 lemon slice

½ cup brown sugar

½ cup water

½ cup red wine

½ pound assorted mixed dried fruits

1. Place the cinnamon, lemon, brown sugar, water, and wine in the pressure cooker and mix well. Select the Sauté function if using an electric pressure cooker or place over medium heat if using a stovetop cooker. Bring to a boil for 6 minutes, then let simmer for 5 minutes.

2. Mix in the dried fruits, seal shut, select the High Pressure function and let cook for 6 minutes.

3. Use the natural release method and slowly remove the lid once the pressure has left the cooker. Serve when ready.

GO PALEO! Replace the brown sugar with ¼ cup natural maple syrup.

PRESSURE-COOKER CHOCOLATE CAKE

MAKES 6-INCH CAKE ◆ PREP TIME: 15 MINUTES ◆ COOKING TIME: 45 MINUTES

For a quick and relatively easy chocolate fix, bake your delicious chocolate cake in your pressure cooker. And for a fudgey center, consider removing the cake several minutes before finished!

3 tablespoons butter, softened

½ cup sugar

1 egg

¼ cup water

3 tablespoons cocoa powder

½ teaspoon vanilla extract

¼ cup milk

¾ cups plain flour

¾ teaspoons baking soda

¼ teaspoon salt

1. In a bowl, whisk together the butter and sugar until the mixture is consistent. Add the egg, beat well, and whisk until the mixture is fluffy.

2. Stir in the water and cocoa powder. Once fully mixed, repeat with the vanilla extract. Repeat again with the milk. Set aside.

3. In a separate bowl, whisk together the flour, baking soda, and salt until the mixture is consistent. Add half of the mixture to the first bowl, stirring sparingly and until there are no large bumps and no flour visible in the batter. Repeat with the second half of the flour mixture.

4. Add the mixture to a greased 6-inch cake pan. Gently tap the cake pan a few times to be sure that no air bubbles remain in the batter.

5. Place a pot stand at the bottom of the pressure cooker, place the cake pan on top of that, close the lid, and select the Low Pressure function. Let cook for 45 minutes or until a toothpick can be inserted into the cake and come out clean. Let cool in the cake pan for 10 to 15 minutes before removing.

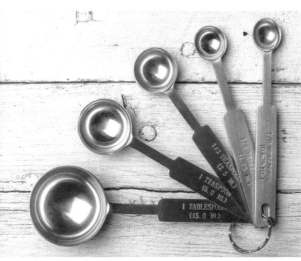

INDEX

ABOUT THE AUTHOR

Jake Grogan is a Fordham University alum who currently lives in Astoria, Queens. Cooking is his favorite hobby, followed by writing. He is the author of *Wit & Wisdom of Camping* and *Wit & Wisdom of the Cowboys*, and when he's not in the kitchen he can be found reviewing new restaurants in New York City and wishing that he had a dog.

ABOUT CIDER MILL PRESS
BOOK PUBLISHERS

Good ideas ripen with time. From seed to harvest, Cider Mill Press brings
fine reading, information, and entertainment together between the covers
of its creatively crafted books. Our Cider Mill bears fruit twice a year,
publishing a new crop of titles each spring and fall.

"Where Good Books Are Ready for Press"

Visit us on the Web at
www.cidermillpress.com
or write to us at
PO Box 454
Kennebunkport, Maine 04046